THE GOSPELS SPEAK

the Gospels Speak

Addressing Life's Questions

Dorothy A. Lee

Paulist Press
New York / Mahwah, NJ

Cover image *Symbols of the four Evangelists* courtesy of Wikimedia Commons. Artist unknown.
Cover design by Tamian Wood
Book design by Lynn Else

Library of Congress Cataloging-in-Publication Data
Names: Lee, Dorothy A., author.
Title: The Gospels speak : addressing life's questions / Dorothy A. Lee.
Description: New York : Paulist Press, 2017. | Includes bibliographical references.
Identifiers: LCCN 2016030868| ISBN 9780809153244 (pbk. : alk. paper) | ISBN 9781587686658 (ebook)
Subjects: LCSH: Bible. Gospels--Criticism, interpretation, etc. | Suffering—Biblical teaching. | Good and evil—Biblical teaching. | Fear—Biblical teaching. | Life—Biblical teaching. | Symbolism in the Bible.
Classification: LCC BS2555.52 .L43 2017 | DDC 226/.06—dc23 LC record available at https://lccn.loc.gov/2016030868

ISBN 978-0-8091-5324-4 (paperback)
ISBN 978-1-58768-665-8 (e-book)

Published by Paulist Press
997 Macarthur Boulevard
Mahwah, New Jersey 07430

www.paulistpress.com

Printed and bound in the
United States of America

for
Jemima Joan and Theodore Edwin

CONTENTS

FOREWORD

If the subject of a spate of recent publications is a valid indicator, there is a growing trend in recent biblical scholarship to appreciate that the New Testament contains four Gospels and not just one. In fact, this is a venerable conviction of Christianity dating back to the apostolic Church that resisted the harmonization of the four Gospels into one unified account. Although such gospel harmonies were attempted, such as that of Tatian's *Diatesseron* and, to an extent, the efforts of Marcion, they did not prevail. Marcion apparently wanted to create an omnibus gospel narrative—similar to that of Luke—and one with what he considered inappropriate elements omitted.

But the Christian instincts of the early Church stood by a fourfold Gospel solution. The existence of four Gospel accounts as part of the Christian Scriptures was not a decision of the evangelists themselves, even though there seems to have been awareness, at least in the case of Matthew, Luke, and perhaps John, that they were composing a new gospel different from their predecessor (and model?) Mark, since they used this Gospel as a source for their own narrative. But the retaining of a fourfold Gospel was a corporate decision of the early Church after the composition of the Gospels, taken over time and ratified in multiple decisions of local Christian communities that ultimately accepted these four Gospels as normative and not others.

Some modern interpreters portray this process of selection, which we call the formation of the canon, as something of an ecclesiastical conspiracy. Ecclesiastical leaders, in cahoots with imperial authority, feared the more creative expressions of Christian faith found in the noncanonical texts and suppressed their creativity less they be a threat to their Church authority and control. Such a scenario sounds too modern and fits better into the murky fictional world of Dan Brown's novels! While ecclesiastical authority did—and should—have some say in judging the validity of a purported sacred text, much more important was the reception of such texts by multiple local Christian communities and the use of such texts in their worship and catechesis. These Christians recognized in these narratives the Jesus in whom they placed their faith and his teaching that inspired their lives.

There is another recent debate going on whether the evangelists wrote solely for a local community or group of communities, or whether they intended from the outset that their accounts of Jesus' life and mission should be read more widely across the Church. It is hard to settle this debate definitively but it seems more probable that the evangelists wrote primarily for a local audience, but the compelling credible nature of their accounts—which drew deeply on the traditions and collective memory of the early Church—were quickly circulated from community to community. It was this process and the favorable reception of these texts into the life of communities of faith that revealed their inspired and authoritative character. Looked at from the vantage point of faith, this is where the influence of the Spirit within the Christian community did its work.

This may seem like a long "fore-word" to introduce this beautifully written and rich pastoral study of the four Gospels. But, in fact, the fundamental premise of Dorothy Lee's work *The Gospels Speak* is that the diversity, as well as the unity of the gospel witness, is grounded in an appreciation of the fourfold Gospel. Forged in their own unique circumstances, drawing on traditions about Jesus and his disciples alive in their churches, and proclaimed through the literary skill and storytelling capacity of the evangelists, each of the Gospels portrays Jesus and the meaning of Christian life in a distinct way. At the same time, their witness is not contradictory or autonomous; each of the four Gospels authentically portrays the Jesus Christ of Christian faith. This is what enables a skilled and faithful interpreter, like Dorothy Lee, to bring to each Gospel questions—drawn from human experience and deep faith—that can match the characteristic strengths and particular colorization of each Gospel. Thus

Mark, a Gospel forged in suffering and the assault of evil, can be interrogated about the meaning of human suffering; Matthew, a Gospel striking out into a new phase of history, is armed with Jesus' words about trust in God and avoiding toxic or paralyzing fear and anxiety; John, a Gospel that centers on the quest for the God revealed in Jesus, the Word made flesh, can speak to questions of human longing and the search for meaning; and Luke, in his Gospel and in the Acts of the Apostles, enables the Christian to ask about the vast purpose of human life and the arc of history, and how our prayers can be meaningful in connecting us to God's ways of salvation. Indeed, the Gospels do "speak."

There is another debated issue in modern biblical interpretation that stands at the heart of this pastorally rich book on the Gospels. And this has to do with the relevance of the biblical witness for our lives today. As Dorothy Lee affirms, "We read the Bible as part of a centuries-long dialogue between its own diverse and untidy contents and the ever-changing questions and needs of our own cultures....The main point is that the Bible, for all that, belongs to an ancient and alien culture, far behind us in space and time, and still has the remarkable capacity to speak to us today across the centuries" (conclusion). Not all biblical scholars would agree with such a perspective. Many would be much more comfortable dealing with the biblical texts solely as interesting cultural and literary artifacts, as classic religious texts from another world without meaning for contemporary experience. But as the distinguished dean of a school of theology, as an ordained minister of the gospel, and even more important, as evidently a person of deep faith and strong pastoral instincts, Dorothy Lee is not afraid to bring the Gospels into dialogue with profound questions of meaning, questions that, despite the span of history, course through the Scriptures and through our own lives today.

In his powerful assessment of biblical scholarship, *Verbum Domini* (The Word of the Lord), written in response to the 2008 General Synod of the Catholic Church on the "Sacred Scriptures in the Life and Mission of the Church," Pope Benedict validated the use of the historical critical method and other modern methodologies in the exploration of the Bible. But he also emphasized that for a scholar who is a believing Christian, more is required.

The work of authentic Christian scholarship must ultimately also serve the community of faith. This compelling study of the meaning of the Gospels by Dorothy Lee surely fulfills that service in an admirable way.

Donald Senior, CP
President Emeritus and Professor of New Testament
Catholic Theological Union, Chicago, Illinois

PREFACE

This book arose out of years of teaching the Gospels within and beyond the academy, and listening to the kinds of questions raised by students, people in parishes and Church agencies, and those on the margins or outside the Church. It arose out of a sense of frustration that the true riches of the Gospels are at least undervalued if not unknown. It is not a study of hermeneutical principles, although a number of these are clearly implied. Rather, it looks at specific issues that contemporary people struggle with in their own lives, and addresses these questions to the Gospels, to see how they respond and what they might have to offer.

The book does not assume that the Bible has all the answers or that those answers are simply and easily extracted. Biblical interpretation always involves struggle and incompleteness, difficulties in understanding and interpreting the text, and questions that remain frustratingly unanswered. It takes the view, however, that the Bible—the Gospels, in particular—has vital answers to offer: not to cover all the questions we ask, and sometimes to take our questions in unexpected and even disturbing directions. But there are answers, of a kind, and we are left with an impoverished, if not distorted, understanding of Christian faith if we do not hear or heed them. It is precisely the comfort and the challenge of the Gospels that this study seeks to unfold.

In writing this book, I acknowledge with thanks those who have given me inspiration and showed enthusiasm along the way. I am grateful for the support of Trinity College and the Faculty of the Theological School, which gave me the study leave and the encouragement to pursue and complete the project. Two scholars and Church leaders in particular, Professor Christiaan

Mostert and Dr. Muriel Porter, offered wise counsel and advice at various points. Thanks also to Dr. Peter Campbell and Dr. Miriam Nicholls for their perceptive and insightful reading of the manuscript. I am also deeply grateful to Paul McMahon of Paulist Press for his continual support and guidance.

Special thanks go to my immediate family, especially Miriam and Philip (to whose children this book is dedicated), and Irene. Final thanks are due to Quentin Blake and Hildegard, two miniature daschunds, who resisted the sometimes overpowering urge (for them) to destroy the manuscript, as they have done with a number of other theological tomes.

Epiphany, 2016

INTRODUCTION

ARE THERE ANSWERS?

Those who make it their profession to study the Bible are sometimes accused of living in ivory towers, unconnected to the struggles, hopes, and fears of ordinary people. This is particularly said of biblical studies since the Enlightenment, which has become an increasingly technical discipline with methods and terminology that lie beyond the scope of the average reader or churchgoer.

This book is an attempt to make vital connections with the Gospels: between our contemporary human experience and the ancient Word of God. It is not, thank God, an isolated venture. But it is an endeavor to bring a number of contemporary, existential questions to bear on the narratives of the Gospels in order to garner whatever theological wisdom and insights they have to offer us.

It may seem a bold thing to speak of the Gospels having "answers" to some, if not all, of the existential questions thrown up by our lives: questions to do with suffering, evil, meaning, purpose, and prayer. It might appear to imply something facile, as if an answer can be easily accessed and more easily applied to the dilemmas and issues we face. Or it might suggest that the questions can be quickly resolved or lightly dismissed as if they were of no moment, so obvious and so soon settled that they are hardly worth the mention.

Some might even go as far as to say that the questions are more important than the answers, that the journey matters more than the destination, and that the means we choose to employ are of greater significance than the goal. As a guard against facile answers, this is an important point to bear in mind. It reminds us that answers imply questions and that the questions themselves need to be explored, lived, refined before any answer is possible.

At the same time, to say that the answers are less relevant than the questions leaves us in nowhere land. Existential questions without answer, an everlasting journey without destination, the pursuit of means that never reach an end are a recipe for eternal frustration. Finally, the questions themselves will fade into nonbeing. For human life to thrive without falling into despondency and meaninglessness there needs to be some form of answer, some hearing of a voice responding to our cries of bewilderment and longing, the impression of an endpoint that has been and can still be attained.

Yet the objection is helpful for all of that. If it saves us from being facile and omniscient, then that is a good thing. Christian faith does not pretend to solve all the problems of human existence.[1] Its very emphasis on faith indicates that it does not have all the answers to our questions and dilemmas. Instead, it invites trust in a God who does know, a God who hears, and a God who responds, both now and in the age to come. We do not come with a ready-made armory of answers to distribute on street corners. We come first with a listening ear, and then with a modest attempt to speak what we know and believe, admitting all along what we do not know.

For that and other reasons, this book is an endeavor to offer answers to some questions. It is not a comprehensive study of the questions themselves, written either by a philosopher or a psychologist or a social anthropologist or a historian. It is a New Testament perspective, and it is limited to the four Gospels. It is written from a Christian perspective that takes seriously what the Gospels have to say.

THE QUESTIONS

The book revolves around four large, existential questions that profoundly affect people's lives, both in their everyday experience and their apprehension of ultimate reality.

1. How do we respond to evil, suffering, and death, and their presence in our lives? Can we explain them or find freedom from them?
2. How can we free our lives of fear and anxiety in a world that is becoming more and more fearful and fear filled, in a world where mental illness and anxiety are on the increase?
3. What personal meaning can we find in our lives to sustain and nurture us, in and beyond the everyday connections? How do we recognize and respond to the longing for something beyond the everyday, for a deeper connection?
4. What, if anything, can we say of an overall purpose to history and the world's existence, and what part can we play in that purpose? Do our prayers count for anything in the divine plan?

This book does not attempt to interrogate each Gospel on each of these four questions; one question is addressed to one Gospel only. The particular Gospel is carefully chosen as one that is especially apt for the question asked of it. Sometimes the choice may seem obvious—like suffering and the Gospel of Mark or history and the Gospel of Luke. This selection needs to be justified. Why, for example, choose the Gospel of Matthew to discuss fear and anxiety, when the theme can be found in all the Gospels? As we will discover, Matthew has a rather winsome way of addressing this issue, even though he is not unique in taking seriously the disciples' fears and anxieties. Sometimes too the language of our questions finds no direct rejoinder in the biblical text, such as the quest for meaning that is addressed to the Gospel of John. Nowhere does John, or the New Testament as a whole, speak of "meaning." But that does not imply there is no answering echo, no similar concept in the Johannine story, or that our quest for meaning finds no response in that gospel of life.

There are advantages and disadvantages to this approach. The disadvantage is that it ignores other biblical texts that have something significant to offer to each of these questions. All the Gospels have some contribution to make on all the questions, as do other parts of the New Testament: the Letters of Paul, Hebrews, and Revelation. The advantage is that it enables us, rather than flitting freely from text to text without concern for the narrative context, to explore one theme in one Gospel. It allows each gospel narrative to speak, and to speak freely and clearly, in its own terms and from its own perspective. Given the way in which we tend to forage through the Bible for helpful texts and isolate them, this approach attempts to take seriously the entire book and allow its answers to emerge through its narrative and imagery.[2]

THE NATURE OF THE GOSPELS

Before launching into this study, we need to pay attention to the nature of the Gospels themselves, although it will in part emerge from our explorations in each chapter. If we want answers from the gospel texts, we need to know how to read them: what they are and what they are not; how, when, and why they were written; what we know about them and what we do not know; and where we can only make what are hopefully intelligent guesses. There is no unanimity on any of these questions, but there is a consensus of agreement on some of them, and it is worth setting that out before we begin.

The Gospels, as we will see, are not quite the simple writings of Galilean fishermen with limited education and artless style, their message plain for all to see. It is true they possess simplicity of language, especially the Gospels of Matthew, Mark, and John, and they are accessible to anyone who can read and grasp something of their meaning. But they are also highly complex texts, dependent on earlier traditions and writings about which we can only speculate, and they stand in rather confusing and intriguing relationship to one another. To quarry their riches, we need to know something of these issues and that inter-relationship.[3]

Some years ago, there was a good deal of skepticism about whether the Gospels were engaged in writing history or biography; the answer at that stage was that they were neither. In more recent years, however, study of ancient history and ancient biography has demonstrated that the Gospels belong within these genres and would have been recognized as such in the ancient world.[4] This recognition helps us better understand the Gospels. They are not intended as objective, historical accounts of Jesus, written from a neutral perspective. Grounded in history, they nonetheless interpret the events of Jesus' life and death from within their own context, through the lens of the resurrection. They are "Christology in narrative form," and we study them in order to see how "each author tries to portray his understanding of Jesus."[5]

At this point, we confront a considerable difference between our world and that of the ancient world that produced the Gospels. Though books were written in that world and a book trade existed, publication in the ancient world usually meant, first and foremost, oral performance.[6] Most of the Gospels' earliest readers were in fact hearers, and the evangelists wrote for people to hear rather than read: "Let anyone with ears to hear listen" (Mark 4:9).

Reading and writing were, in any case, much more difficult and costly than they are today. The earliest manuscripts of the Gospels were most likely dictated and written by specialist secretaries on parchment or papyrus scrolls (and later, on codices—which means books). These manuscripts have little, if any, punctuation and no spacing between the words. The "reader" of a Gospel, in ancient terms, is technically the person reading aloud to a group of listeners and has to be well prepared for the task.[7] There are no chapter and verse divisions in the early documents, as these came much later.[8]

In these and other ways, the world of the Gospels represents a very different culture from Western culture. In some ways, the biblical world is closer to cultures today that are least affected by Western ways. It is a social culture that values the family and community over the individual, a psychological culture in which individual identity is always embedded in relationship with others and particularly family, a gendered culture in which men belong in the public sphere and pursue honor while women are confined to the private sphere,[9] their core virtue being shame.[10] It is at best a semiliterate culture in which most people cannot read or write, and where life-and-death issues are debated in the public square, the marketplace, the center of community life.[11]

Judaism is a religious culture that sees human life as caught up in a cosmic battle between transcendent forces beyond the natural realm.

Within that world, it is most likely that the Gospels are rather late writings in the New Testament. These days, they are usually dated to the second or third generation, somewhere between AD 60 and 100, which is later than, for example, the Pauline Letters. The Gospel of Mark is generally considered to be the earliest of the Gospels, written perhaps a decade or so before any of the others. This view constitutes a challenge to the traditional perspective on Mark's Gospel, which sees it as the abbreviator of Matthew and thus of lesser comparable value.[12] The belief in Markan priority—Mark as the first Gospel to be written—finds a remarkable consensus among biblical scholars today, though it is not unanimous and there is still a very small minority who support the traditional view of the priority of Matthew's Gospel.

The main critical issue with the Gospels is the "Synoptic problem," the problem associated with the close interrelationship between the first three Gospels. In fact, the problem arises because of the Gospel of John and its marked difference from the other three Gospels at a number of points. Without John, we might well assume that Jesus' ministry lasted approximately one year, that he visited Jerusalem only once as an adult, and that the centerpiece of his ministry was his journey to Jerusalem, during which he prophesied his impending arrest in Jerusalem, his suffering, death, and resurrection.

But, in fact, John presents a rather different scenario, one in which Jesus visits Jerusalem three times (that is, over three years), once being early in his ministry. Most scholars suggest a later dating, sometime in the last decade of the first century. The Johannine Jesus cleanses the temple at the beginning of his ministry, not at the end, as with the Synoptics (John 2:13–22). We see the Johannine Jesus moving from Cana in Galilee to Jerusalem and then back to Cana, via Samaria (2:1—4:54). While the overall schema is the same in all four Gospels—a ministry beginning with John the Baptist, continuing in Galilee and Judea, and concluding in Jerusalem with Jesus' death and resurrection—the Johannine ministry moves between Galilee and Judea and encompasses three yearly Passover feasts (2:13; 6:4; 13:1), instead of the Synoptic solitary Passover at the Last Supper (Mark 14:1).

A number of the stories differ, along with some of the major characters. There are no exorcisms in John's Gospel, and Jesus' ministry begins and ends with miracles unknown to the Synoptics: the changing of water into wine at Cana (2:1–11) and the raising of Lazarus from the dead (11:1–44); the foot-washing is likewise unique to John (13:1–20). While Peter is an important figure, Andrew and Philip have greater prominence than the Synoptic counterparts. Other characters are unique to John— Nicodemus, the man born blind, and Lazarus—and women play a key role as disciples: the mother of Jesus, the Samaritan woman, Martha and Mary of Bethany, and Mary Magdalene. At the same time, various Synoptic stories are perhaps surprisingly absent: the baptism of Jesus in water, the transfiguration, and the institution of the Eucharist. That leaves us with the conclusion that the first three Gospels are closely intertwined, and that their narrative perspective is as much guided by theological considerations as that of John's Gospel.

Once Markan chronological priority is established, it follows that both Matthew and Luke have employed Mark in the construction of their Gospels. That explains the commonality among the three in structure, narrative, metaphor, characterization, and theological focus. Luke, in any case, makes it plain that he is not the first to write in this mode and that he has benefitted from the efforts of others (Luke 1:1–3). Given his self-awareness as a historian, we might expect that, in the terms of his own day, Luke has engaged in research before writing his Gospel. Many scholars believe, moreover, that both Matthew and Luke had access to a common source consisting of the sayings of Jesus, since both have common sayings not found in Mark and yet placed in very different locations in each Gospel.[13]

As for John, for a period of time in the twentieth century, this Gospel was considered independent of the first three, the Synoptic Gospels. More recently, however, there has been increasing interest in the common ground that exists among the first three Gospels and the Gospel of John. This commonality suggests to some the direct use of Mark or one other of the Gospels in the writing of John—with the intent of supplementing or correcting the Synoptics—or at least the use of similar traditions and signs of early cross-fertilization.[14] The actual degree of separation is something that has been debated almost from the beginning and intensely so since the Enlightenment. The early Church saw John as the interpreter of Matthew, Mark, and Luke, familiar with them but complementing and, in a sense, "theologizing" them—the "spiritual Gospel," as it was sometimes called.[15]

We refer to these writings as "Gospels" and we do so, in part, because Mark begins his by describing it as "gospel" or "good news": "The beginning of the good news [gospel] of Jesus Christ, the Son of God" (Mark 1:1). Luke, by contrast, describes his work as an "orderly account" or "narrative" (Luke 1:1). But the main reason we call them "Gospels" is because that is what they are called in Church Tradition, where we distinguish between the Gospels as formal writings and the message itself of the "gospel," the good news of Jesus Christ.

But perhaps we need to be more accurate at this point. In the early manuscripts, each of the Gospels begins with a superscription containing only the phrase and the name, "According to…" In other words, in the ancient traditions, there is really one G/gospel and we have four versions of it: the version according to Matthew, the version according to Mark, the version according to Luke, and the version according to John. This division from a single designation, "Gospel," implies that, for the early Church, there was a unity within the fourfold Gospel, a unity that one of the early Fathers compares to the four winds of heaven and the four corners of the earth.[16]

Modern readings of the Gospels tend to emphasize the differences among them, and note that John is particularly different from the first three Gospels, which share, as we have noted, a common structure and similar stories. Since the Enlightenment, considerable work has been done comparing the Gospels to one another, and observing the points of agreement and disagreement. Part of this endeavor has been to gain a sense of each evangelist as a distinctive storyteller and theologian in his own right. The emphasis on difference has helped us to see a depth of richness in that diversity, and a theological breadth we had never before fully grasped.

It is as if each Gospel is viewing a mountain from a different angle—the first three not far from each other in stance and position, and John from the opposite side of the mountain. Nonetheless, it is still the same mountain, however many positions there are from which to view it. This diversity need not rule out an overarching unity in the presentation of Jesus as the Son of God who brings the life and reign of God to bear on human life in order to rescue it from sin, evil, suffering, meaninglessness, and death, and in the rise of the Christian community from Jesus' life and ministry, death, and resurrection.

Traditionally, each Gospel has been associated with a symbolic creature from Revelation in its introductory vision of worship and the heavenly sanctuary:

> Around the throne, and on each side of the throne, are four living creatures, full of eyes in front and behind: the first living creature like a lion, the second living creature like an ox, the third living creature with a face like a human face, and the fourth living creature like a flying eagle. And the four living creatures, each of them with six wings, are full of eyes all around and inside. (Rev 4:6–8; see Ezek 10)

In later Church Tradition, Matthew is associated with the human being, stressing the human face of Jesus as Emmanuel ("God with us") in this Gospel; Mark is the winged lion, signifying the power of his words in the Gospel; Luke is the winged ox, symbol of sacrifice but also the sheer strength of a beast of burden, given his emphasis on the poor and needy; and John is symbolized by the eagle, the bird that soars high into the spiritual heavens.[17] These symbols help to locate the distinct contribution each has to make, though in Revelation, the four living creatures are together around the divine throne, worshipping God and the Lamb (Rev 5:8–10). The symbols establish both the union among the Gospels and their remarkable differences.

THE SHAPE OF THIS BOOK

We begin each chapter in this study with a brief analysis of the question to be addressed, with a wider awareness of the biblical world in which it resonates, and particularly the Old Testament influence. That leads into some background material on how to read the particular Gospel and why, specifically, it has been chosen. There follows an outline of the theme, or themes, as it or they appear throughout the Gospel, taking seriously the narrative form and not simply quarrying it for meaning. Finally, we interrogate the Gospel from our perspective to see what it offers our contemporary context.

The order of chapters does not reflect the canonical order, nor, necessarily, the order in which the books were most likely written. We begin with the Gospel of Mark and the question of evil, death, and suffering. The next chapter examines Matthew—closest in content and form to Mark—and the question of how we deal with fear and anxiety. The third chapter explores John and the question of personal meaning that is to be found in the Fourth Gospel's understanding of eternal life and discipleship. Fourth, broadening the question of meaning, we turn to the Gospel of Luke for an understanding of the divine purpose that lies within history and the question of our participation in that purpose.

Notes

1. The Archbishop of Canterbury said in an interview in 2014, "We can't explain all the questions in the world, we can't explain about suffering, we can't explain loads of things but we know about Jesus." See "Standing Room Only: Interview with Archbishop Justin Welby," https://www.youtube.com/watch?v=exmHYXNEt9A&feature=youtu.be&t=11m52s.

2. Reputable modern translations of the Bible include, within the tradition of the King James Version, the New Revised Standard Version (an ecumenical translation) and the English Standard Version (an Evangelical translation, though without use of inclusive language). Outside the KJV tradition are the standard New Jerusalem Bible (Roman Catholic) and the New

International Version (Evangelical). The translation used here, unless otherwise indicated, is the NRSV.

3. A good introduction to the Gospels is Mark Allan Powell, *Fortress Introduction to the Gospels* (Minneapolis: Augsburg Fortress, 1998); and to the New Testament as a whole is Pheme Perkins, *Reading the New Testament: An Introduction*, 3rd ed. (Mahwah, NJ: Paulist Press, 2012).

4. See especially, Richard A. Burridge, *What Are the Gospels? A Comparison with Graeco-Roman Biography*, 2nd ed. (Grand Rapids: Eerdmans, 2004), 185–251.

5. Richard A. Burridge, *Four Gospels, One Jesus? A Symbolic Reading*, 2nd ed. (Grand Rapids: Eerdmans, 2005), 8.

6. Loveday Alexander, "Ancient Book Production and the Circulation of the Gospels," in *The Gospels for All Christians: Rethinking the Gospel Audiences*, ed. Richard Bauckham (Edinburgh: T & T Clark, 1998), 86–87. For a reflection on a modern oral performance of Mark, see David Rhoads, *Reading Mark: Engaging the Gospel* (Minneapolis: Fortress, 2004), 176–201.

7. On literacy in the ancient world, see E. Randolph Richards, "Reading, Writing, and Manuscripts," in *The World of the New Testament: Cultural, Social, and Historical Contexts*, ed. Joel B. Green and Lee Martin McDonald (Grand Rapids: Baker Academic, 2013), 345–66.

8. Chapter divisions were added in the thirteenth century, and these were later subdivided into verses in the sixteenth century. They are not necessarily a reliable guide for structural divisions.

9. The actual reality, for women, was probably much more ambiguous and diverse than this simple statement suggests.

10. On honor-shame values (from a modern African perspective that has parallels with the ancient world), see, for example, Elijah Malangu, "The Ancient Mediterranean Values of Honour and Shame as a Hermeneutical Procedure," *Verbum et Ecclesia* 22 (2001): 85–101.

11. On the Greco-Roman and Jewish worlds of the New Testament, see Bart D. Ehrman, *The New Testament: A Historical Introduction to the Early Christian Writings*, 4th ed. (New York: Oxford University Press, 2008), 17–55.

12. See Joel Marcus, *Mark 1–8: A New Translation with Introduction and Commentary* (New York: Doubleday, 2000), 40–47.

13. Not all scholars accept the existence of Q, the hypothetical sayings source. The main alternative, while accepting the priority of Mark, is that Luke had access to both Mark and Matthew in the composing of his Gospel. For the arguments for and against Q, see David Sloan, "The Case for Q," http://www. umass.edu/wsp/alpha/forum/luke/2014e%20Sloan%20Q%20 abs.pdf; and Mark Goodacre, "Ten Reasons to Question Q," http://www.markgoodacre.org/Q/ten.htm.

14. See, for example, Paul N. Anderson, *The Fourth Gospel and the Quest for Jesus: Modern Foundations Reconsidered* (London: T & T Clark, 2006).

15. The description comes from Clement of Alexandria (c. 150–215), quoted in Eusebius, *Ecclesiastical History* 6.14.5–7.

16. Irenaeus, *Against Heresies*, 3.11.8: "The Gospels could not possibly be either more or less in number than they are. Since there are four zones of the world in which we live, and four principal winds, while the Church is spread over all the earth, and the pillar and foundation of the Church is the gospel, and the Spirit of life, it fittingly has four pillars, everywhere breathing out incorruption and revivifying men." (Cyril Richardson, *Early Christian Fathers* [New York, NY: Touchstone, 1996], 382.)

17. Further on these symbols in relation to the four Gospels, see Burridge, *Four Gospels*, 34–163.

Chapter 1

SUFFERING AND EVIL
AND THE GOSPEL
OF MARK

CONTEXT

Why do suffering and evil exist in the world? This is perhaps the quintessential question of our age. We live in a world characterized by suffering, violence, injustice, disease, and death. The last one hundred years and more have been perhaps the most bloody of all time, and despite the advances in medical and technological knowledge, diseases new and old continue to bring human lives to untimely ends. Natural disasters have claimed the lives of millions, and the planet itself is showing distressing signs of suffering through climate change.

Too often for our comfort, the forces that inflict evil and oppression have won out over the good intentions and courageous actions of human beings. And death seems to be the final statement on our lives, and indeed on all life. We face the reality not only of our own death but also that of our planet.

The issues are hardly new. Writers and poets have written of them, from religious to agnostic to atheist, from the ancient world to the modern. For many people, the problem of pain is precisely the reason they doubt, or reject altogether, the existence of God—including those who have been, at one stage, Christian believers.[1] Suffering is one of the two great barriers to belief in a

1

good God; the other is materialism, the conviction that the fulsome and comforting materiality of our world is all there is.

The actor and writer Stephen Fry, an avowed atheist, was asked in an interview with an Irish journalist what he would say if he were to meet God. His answer is chilling yet compelling, raising sharply the question of suffering and evil:

> I'll say, "Bone cancer in children? What's that about? How dare you! How dare you create a world where there is such misery that is not our fault! It's not right. It is utterly, utterly evil. Why should I respect a capricious, mean-minded, stupid god who creates a world that is so full of injustice and pain....Yes, the world is very splendid, but it also has in it insects whose whole life-cycle is to burrow into the eyes of children and make them blind. They eat outwards from the eyes. Why did you do that? Why? Why did you do that to us? You could easily have made a creation where that didn't exist. It is simply not acceptable." So, you know, atheism is not just about not believing there's a god— but, on the assumption there is one, what kind of god is it? It's perfectly apparent that he is monstrous, utterly monstrous, and deserves no respect whatsoever. The moment you banish him, your life becomes simpler, purer, cleaner—more worth living in my opinion.[2]

Fry is not alone in his concerns. Christian thinkers have also engaged with the question. Indeed, there is a whole branch of theology dedicated to this question, called "theodicy." For example, C. S. Lewis's famous book *The Problem of Pain* deals with the intellectual issues of how suffering can be equated with Christian belief in divine goodness and omnipotence (including in the animal kingdom). Lewis begins his study by setting out succinctly his own objections to God's existence in his former, atheist days, a response based on human suffering and transience:

> The creatures cause pain by being born, and live by inflicting pain, and in pain they mostly die....[Human] history is largely a record of crime, war, disease, and

terror, with just sufficient happiness interposed to give them, while it lasts, an agonized apprehension of losing, and, when it is lost, the poignant misery of remembering…all civilisations pass away and, even while they remain, inflict peculiar sufferings of their own… all life will turn out in the end to have been a transitory and senseless contortion upon the idiotic face of infinite matter.[3]

It is one thing to reason about the place and purpose of suffering as a Christian, and quite another thing to endure it personally. Later in his life, Lewis recorded his own intense grief at the loss of his beloved wife and the love that came to him late in life. At one point, in this context, he writes of the added misery human consciousness makes to raw suffering:

Part of every misery is, so to speak, the misery's shadow or reflection: the fact that you don't merely suffer but have to keep on thinking about the fact that you suffer. I not only live each endless day in grief, but live each thinking about living each day in grief.[4]

This experience of grief leads Lewis at first to agonizing doubts about his faith—not primarily about the existence of God as such, but rather about the goodness and consoling presence of God. Later, as he comes to terms with his own suffering, he can look back and see how grief has shaken his intellectual world and left it looking threadbare and trite.

Christians do not believe there are easy answers to the problem of evil and suffering. It is true that Christian theology has a worldview that refuses to sweep aside evil and suffering but, on the contrary, endeavors to set it, like C. S. Lewis, within a cogent understanding of a saving, self-revealing God. There are versions of Christianity, however, that exacerbate the problem of suffering by confidently "explaining" a tragic event as the divine punishment of individual or social sin—a monstrous God, indeed.

THE RESPONSE OF THE BIBLE

The Bible itself is acutely aware of the problem of evil and suffering. There is perhaps no more powerful statement of suffering and evil than this plaintive lament from the psalmist: "How long, O Lord? Will you forget me forever? / How long will you hide your face from me? / How long must I bear pain in my soul, / and have sorrow in my heart all day long? How long shall my enemy be exalted over me?" (Ps 13:1–2). Or this from another psalm: "My God, my God, why have you forsaken me? / Why are you so far from helping me, from the words of my groaning? / O my God, I cry by day, but you do not answer; / and by night, but find no rest" (Ps 22:1–2).

Nor is there a more powerful story of undeserved suffering in the Old Testament than that of Job who famously loses everything—his wealth, health, and family—at the hands of Satan. Job's unjust suffering is exacerbated by the friends who are convinced he has sinned and needs only to repent and accept divine judgment. But Job tenaciously confirms his innocence while bewailing his fate and cursing the day of his birth, though never actually cursing God: "My sighing comes like my bread, / and my groanings are poured out like water. / Truly the thing that I fear comes upon me, / and what I dread befalls me. / I am not at ease, nor am I quiet; / I have no rest; but trouble comes" (Job 3:24–26).

Job's story is set within an Old Testament religious context that understands sin as a primary cause of suffering in human life. In the biblical world, sin results from the failure to live out the life-giving law of God, which promotes justice, holiness, and harmonious relationships, and condemns violence and wrongdoing, even to the stranger and alien. The biblical world highlights the destructive effects and reality of sin, but at the same time is able to question a simplistic connection between sin and suffering. There are realms of suffering beyond that of sin: pain inflicted on the innocent, suffering as the result of inexplicable tragedy, and the ever-present reality of death.

The problem of suffering in the New Testament is accentuated, above all, in Jesus himself and the manner and means of his death: the true and ultimate innocent sufferer.[5] Yet Paul also catalogues his own unjust suffering in his mission:

> Three times I was beaten with rods. Once I received a stoning. Three times I was shipwrecked; for a night and a day I was adrift at sea; on frequent journeys, in danger from rivers, danger from bandits, danger from my own people, danger from Gentiles, danger in the city, danger in the wilderness, danger at sea, danger from false brothers and sisters; in toil and hardship, through many a sleepless night, hungry and thirsty, often without food, cold and naked. (2 Cor 11:25–27)

For Paul, these sufferings represent "the marks of Jesus" that "I carry…on my body" (*stigmata*, Gal 6:17).[6] They are, in a sense, the extension of Christ's own innocent suffering, and they point to an acute awareness of the problem of pain and its inevitability, as well as its enigma, in the present order of things.

The Bible also assumes that human beings have a real choice about how they live and that, behind the choice lies the God-given freedom to choose good or evil. This is built into the order of creation, as the story of the Garden first makes plain. Here human beings are given the freedom to choose: between obedience and disobedience, between life and death. They are neither slaves nor puppets. Christian theology believes that creation itself contains what David Bentley Hart calls "the mystery of created freedom" that enables "the union of free creatures with the God of love" and that implies "the power of creation to enslave itself to death," a freedom donated by God.[7] It is this implicit freedom that underlies biblical understandings of the world and its suffering.

READING MARK ARIGHT

The specific Gospel to which we are addressing these questions is the Gospel of Mark, the earliest and first Gospel to be written—so succinct yet so powerful that two other Gospels took their structure and many of their stories from it. We imagine Mark as the Lion, as his Gospel is usually depicted, but we do not know for certain who the author was or where he lived. Most likely his location is Rome, as tradition suggests, where he was a disciple of Peter, as tradition also suggests.[8] He may have been an anonymous Christian from Northern Palestine, as some have suggested.[9] Or he may have been a bishop in the Church and martyred in Alexandria, and the founder of the Church there, as Coptic Christians believe. Externally, all we have are ancient traditions, dating back to the second century, and scholarly conjectures: few incontrovertible facts and only the beliefs of the early generations, and the speculations of modern scholarship that are based on internal evidence from the text.[10]

We do know that the Gospel itself is a troubled, somewhat ambiguous text. Jesus seems to appear from nowhere, without genealogy or birth; his public ministry is clouded by a reluctance to perform or be known or named;[11] his disciples often fail to understand him; his death is carried out in agonizing pain and an acute sense of abandonment; his resurrection is never encountered except by implication and the bald message of a celestial young man; and the Gospel ends abruptly with the flight and silence of the women disciples from the tomb (16:8).[12]

Yet this is the Gospel we will interrogate, far from us though it may be in space and time, in context and worldview.[13] Some of our questions will be met only with silence, and we need to be prepared for that. To others, Mark will return a blank stare, an unknowing shrug of the shoulders, a slow and sad shaking of the head. He will not answer all our questions, and he will not resolve our own ambiguities, our doubts, our fears.

But he will speak, and we may well be even more amazed at what he says than what he does not say. Amazement, after all, is a feature of this Gospel, and at times its characters, both believing and unbelieving, are amazed at what Jesus says and does, at how he lives and dies, and at who he really is (e.g., 1:27; 5:20; 10:32; 12:17; 15:5). We need, however, to read Mark's Gospel carefully and in its own terms. This reading will involve some discomfort for us, and we will be taken to a world very different from our own, and to a kind of literature that has few direct parallels in our contemporary world.

In the first place, Mark's Gospel is a stylized and carefully interpreted account of Jesus' life and death. It is not exactly history as we might define it, as we observed in the introduction, though the ancient world would probably have recognized it as biography. The ancients did not see the telling of a person's life as a neutral or dispassionate task, but rather an opportunity to draw the moral, to improve the reader's life, to extol virtue and condemn vice, in short, to teach.[14] And Mark's Gospel declares itself, right from the beginning, as a work of proclamation that emphasizes Jesus' preaching and teaching: "the good news of Jesus Christ, the Son of God" (Mark 1:1; cf. 1:14; 1:22). For all its ambiguities in the ensuing narrative, Mark sees himself as bringing good news to the reader: as proclaiming something and someone to transform utterly the reader's (hearer's) life.

As a consequence of a listening rather than a reading public, the structure of Mark's Gospel is very clearly demarcated, not by chapter and verse, which are much later (and more literate) inventions, but by geography and a sense of space and place.[15] After the prologue, which locates Jesus' identity (1:1–15), the ministry takes place in and around Galilee, mostly in Jewish but sometimes also Gentile territory (1:16—8:21). The Markan plot makes a dramatic turning point at Caesarea Philippi, the northernmost point of Jesus' ministry, from where we follow Jesus on the journey to Jerusalem (8:22—10:52). The last chapters revolve around Jerusalem (11:1—16:8), with a final message pointing back to Galilee as the place of Jesus' future risen appearance (16:7).

The structure is not strictly chronological, except in its broad outlines (Jesus' ministry beginning with John the Baptist and ending in Jerusalem with his death on the cross), but it is governed primarily by Mark's theological intent. Only once does Jesus visit Jerusalem in this Gospel (11:11), his ministry set mainly in Galilee. The evangelist uses this geographical structure as both metaphor and theology. The ministry in the Galilean towns and villages is itself symbolic of the future kingdom or reign of God (*basileia*), now anticipated in the healings and teaching, the feeding of the hungry, the bestowal of forgiveness. The fact that at several points the ministry crosses boundaries into Gentile territory, where Jesus' healing and teaching continues, indicates the broadening of God's reign to a universal scope that embraces all people.

The journey to Jerusalem, bounded on either side by the healing of two blind men, one at the beginning and one at the end (8:22–26; 10:46–52), is likewise metaphorical. It signifies the journey of discipleship, "following" Jesus on the cross-bearing, self-denying pathway to suffering and death for the sake of others, for the sake of life. The final week in Jerusalem (11:1—13:37) typifies the conflict between the forces of destruction that can only destroy the truth and those who offer self-sacrificing goodness and love—a conflict in which the forces of death and destruction seem at first glance to win the day.

Each phase of the Gospel, in other words, functions both literally and symbolically. It reenacts the actual ministry of Jesus himself, the wayward response of many of his closest followers, and the rejection by the religious authorities. But it does so in a new context, with a specific interpretation of those events in mind. It does not seek to portray the whole of Jesus' ministry but only those aspects that Mark draws out and reshapes for his own context and community. In doing so, the Gospel depicts—one or two generations after the events it portrays[16]—the journey of faith for contemporary Christians, the hope of God's future, the pathway of the Church's life. Each narrative phase depicts the anticipation of God's reign, the astonishing direction of God's way and the unexpected scope of God's mind, and their significance for the transformation of the readers' (hearers') lives.

With these few markers in mind, we come closer to reading Mark's Gospel within its own interpretative framework. That means primarily within its own theological framework, but we access that theology through knowledge of the Markan world and through awareness of Mark's narrative techniques and literary devices. These are not mere teaching aids to communicate the message, nor are they sugar to coat the medicine. They are themselves the message, a message that is tied inextricably to the gospel narrative. The questions we ask of Mark are prosaic and logical; Mark will answer us through story and imagery.

To read Mark aright thus gives access to a remarkable world that, while being so very different from our own, can nonetheless speak into the heart of contemporary cultures. It is rewarding work to make this effort at reading. Otherwise, we will read Mark only as a mirror of our world, our own desires, our own sense of religious identity, and consequently miss its true riches and transforming power.

THE QUESTIONS

We have already noted that Mark may not have direct answers to our questions, and that the answers may take a very different form from the questions. The questions themselves, after all, may need to be refined in the light of the answers. Questions do not have absolute value, as when a small child asks, "Is three enough?" or "Why is weather?" Question and answer live together, shaping and reshaping each other through dialogue and desire, through mutual listening and understanding.

If we ask Mark, rather bluntly, to explain for us in words of few syllables the problem of suffering, we will be met with a deafening silence. Nowhere does the Gospel of Mark seek to "explain" the existence of evil and suffering in the world. That does not mean, however, that Mark is unaware of the underlying issue. Indeed, Mark's is the Gospel most attuned to suffering and radically confrontative of the powers of evil. Clearly, Mark sees them as fundamental and existential problems in human life, problems that demand resolution.

A theological reading of Mark and his understanding of evil and suffering will also, at the same time, involve the question of sin. At the beginning of the Gospel, John the Baptist's proclamation calls for repentance of sin, of which baptism is the symbol (1:4–5). Baptism is accompanied by confession of sin in those who journey to the Jordan River, and Mark sees baptism and confession as preparation for the coming of the Messiah. Sin, in other words, is part of what is involved in both suffering and evil for Mark. Theologically, in the New Testament, if we speak of these problems, we cannot do so without speaking of the fundamental problem of sin: that destructive and self-destructive impulse in human nature that leads people to acts of selfishness and indifference, greed and violence.

As we read through Mark's Gospel—and our initial reading will not take much more than an hour—we might decide to reframe our questions. What light does Mark shed on the place and ultimate significance of suffering and death? How seriously does he take sin and evil in the world, and how does he present it? In what way are sin, suffering, evil, and death overcome in this Gospel, giving consolation and hope for the reader/hearer, a hope that will transform the present moment?

MARK AND THE POWERS OF EVIL

Mark has undoubtedly a strong focus on evil. The Gospel depicts vividly human suffering from various evils: from disability, disease, hunger, mental illness, alienation, oppression, and of course, sin. A man is excommunicated from his community because of infectious disease (1:40–45). A woman is ostracized because she has endured severe menstrual symptoms for twelve years, with the resultant poverty from expensive (and ineffective) medical treatment, exclusion from community, and physical weakness through loss of blood (5:25–34). A man lies paralyzed and condemned to poverty and inaction (2:1–12). A woman, who happens to be Peter's mother-in-law, is bedridden with a potentially deadly fever (1:30–31). People suffer from blindness and other disabilities (1:32–34). The disciples are in danger of drowning on the seas with the sudden advent of a storm (4:35–51; 6:45–52). People are famished after a day of listening to Jesus' teaching (6:30–43; 8:1–10). A grief-stricken father has just lost his beloved twelve-year-old daughter (5:21–43).[17]

In each case, there is an immediate resolution. Jesus responds miraculously to the afflicted person or persons. In the typical pattern of miracle stories in the Gospels, the physical need is made apparent (illness, disability, danger, hunger, death), and a miracle is requested through the faith of the sufferer or that of his or her friends. Jesus responds at once, accompanying the miracle with a healing or commanding word, often accompanied by physical touch. The success of the miracle is emphasized (it

is usually immediate) and people respond, often with astonishment and sometimes with hostility and unbelief.

Mark's Jesus is unafraid of contact with the sick and the dying. The pollution of infectious disease or the social stigma of uncleanness do not affect him or prevent him touching the sufferer. The sharp opposition between ritually clean and unclean is very much a part of the world of ancient Judaism and quite different from the opposition we make in our culture between "clean" and "dirty." Proximity to blood or semen, touching the dead, contact with animals considered unclean or with those whose lifestyle places them outside the Law render a person unclean until they are ceremonially "cleansed," restored through ritual washing (Lev 11:1—15:33).[18]

Although this ancient opposition of clean/unclean might be understood in positive ways (demonstrating, for example, the holiness of childbirth or the numinous state of the dead, or keeping infectious disease at bay), for Mark, it places grave restrictions on those whose disability, whether moral or ritual, is long-term or even permanent. This social factor is an intrinsic part of the evil of alienation from family and community.

In Mark's Gospel, people can become alienated from community through their lifestyle, whether it be morally reprehensible (such as thieves or prostitutes), socially unacceptable (such as tax collectors who collude with the imperialistic powers of Rome), or simply because they are unable, through various causes, to maintain strict purity rules. Being outside the community is never more clearly expressed than in the refusal of the "righteous" (those within the Law) to eat with "sinners" (those outside the Law), whether Jewish or Gentile. Jesus' table fellowship breaks through these distinctions, inviting the outsiders into communion and sociality around the table (2:15–17)—first for Jewish outsiders, then for Gentiles.

Mark does not use the word group *sin* and *sinner* very often in his Gospel, but the signs of it are present everywhere. It is manifest in the willful misunderstanding of the disciples and their reluctance to grasp God's ways (e.g., 6:52), in the betrayal of Judas, the flight of the disciples, and the denial of Peter (14:66–72). It is even more markedly present in the response of the Jerusalem authorities, who are threatened by Jesus' challenge to

their authority and who scheme with malevolence and cunning to have him put to death (14:1–2). It is also present in the Roman judicial authorities and the gross miscarriage of justice in Jesus' trial, scourging, and crucifixion (15:15).

The relationship between sin and evil is not a simple one. Evil can sometimes transcend the individual; people can be the innocent victims of evil and not the perpetrators. That is certainly the case with the exorcisms where individuals are inhabited by evil powers over which they have no say, no choice, and no power. Mark does not assume in every case—not even in most cases—a direct link between sin and evil. The victims of illness and disability are not blamed for their plight. Yet sin is nonetheless present in and around these narratives: in the anger of the authorities at Jesus' willingness and authority to set people free, in the impatience and misunderstanding of the disciples,[19] and in the absence of grace that marginalizes and excludes.

The healing that Jesus offers deals with an evil that afflicts both body and soul. In one of the early narratives, Mark presents Jesus healing a paralyzed man by first offering him forgiveness of his sins (2:5–9). This story is as much about the hostility that Jesus' offer of forgiveness arouses in the authorities as it is about a healing. Yet the healing is unquestionably holistic: the man is "healed" in body and soul.

Similarly, in two later healings, the woman with the hemorrhage and blind Bartimaeus, Jesus says (literally) to the healed person: "*Your* faith has made you well" (*sôzô*, 5:34, 10:52). The implication of this choice of words—which is literally "your faith has saved you"—is that more has been overcome than simply the healing of a physical complaint. Indeed, both characters in these healings display an extraordinary faith in Jesus, reinforcing the point that something more has happened than a physical healing. In the first case, Jesus addresses the woman as "daughter" (5:34), implying a close relationship between them and, in the second case, Bartimaeus immediately follows Jesus, joining the company of his disciples (10:52). A spiritual healing is also manifest here, a drawing out and confirming of faith.

Death, too, is part of the problem of suffering, death as a significant manifestation of evil both for the deceased and for those who mourn them. There is no doubt that Mark strongly

confirms Jesus' belief in the resurrection of the dead, as is apparent when he predicts to his half-deaf disciples his own resurrection (e.g., 8:31) and in his dispute with the Sadducees, where he undermines their attempt to ridicule the notion of life beyond the grave (12:18–27). Mark makes clear that the tragedy of mortality is not the last word on human life.

In each case, Jesus shows himself responsive to evil and suffering in their various forms, whether physical, mental, or social. He is ready to heal, to feed, to forgive, and to welcome. Whatever evils people experience, and whether or not the blame is theirs, Jesus' response is at once to allay it, and to restore the victims and suppliants to wholeness and forgiveness, safety and satiety, community and life.[20]

MARK'S EXORCISMS

More difficult for modern Western sensibilities is the way that Mark's miracle stories are dominated by exorcisms. The very first miracle of this Gospel is the exorcism of a demon-possessed man in the context of Jesus' teaching (1:21–28). Its prime position in the narrative of Jesus' ministry gives it significant emphasis. In Mark's summaries of Jesus' ministry—and the ministry he will pass on to his disciples when he sends them out on mission (6:7)—exorcisms have a key place. The exorcisms in the story of the Gentile mother of a demon-possessed daughter (7:24–30), and that of the Jewish father of a demon-possessed son (whose symptoms to our eyes seem like epilepsy, 9:14–27), possess an intimate touch. Each has an unusual or even outrageous element, whether it lies in Jesus' initial repulsing of the Gentile Syro-Phoenician women (7:27) or the disciples' surprising inability to heal the epileptic boy and Jesus' sharp criticism of their lack of faith (9:17–19).

But the most dramatic and troubling exorcism is the story of the Gerasene demoniac (5:1–20). The story forms part of a wider narrative demonstrating the build-up of Jesus' words and acts of power, from the parables to the calming of the storm, the exorcism, and the healing of incurable disease and the raising

of the dead (4:1—5:43). Mark presents a vivid contrast between
the demon-possessed man as we first encounter him and the
man as we leave him. Initially, he is alienated in every possible way: from his community, from his own self, from his God.
He is naked, restless, unclean, dangerous, and self-destructive,
avoided by everyone and living a wretched existence among the
tombs (5:3–5); he is also, seemingly, a Gentile. After his encounter with Jesus, however, we see an entirely different picture. Now
he is clothed and in his right mind, sitting quietly and peacefully
beside his healer (5:15). Only Jesus in this Gospel has the power
to heal and make the man whole, restoring him to himself, to his
own community in which he is instructed to remain, and to "the
Lord" who has had mercy on him (5:19).

This much of the Gerasene story we can appreciate; the rest
is puzzling for contemporary readers, already puzzled by exorcisms in the first place.[21] It is hard not to observe that tragedy
accompanies this otherwise heartwarming tale. The exorcism is
brought about at the cost of a whole herd of animals who, mad-
dened by the demons, hurl themselves into the sea and drown,
all two thousand of them (5:11–13). And, in the last scene, the
man's neighbors, far from being delighted at the restoration of
their friend, react instead with fear and promptly ask Jesus to
leave the district (5:17).

Readers have tried to make sense of this strange story by
noting that, for Jewish people, pigs are unclean animals and
therefore their destruction is a matter of indifference to Jesus
and his disciples. Others have thought that the language used by
the demons might suggest metaphorically a battalion of Roman
soldiers, considered an unclean and alien presence in Palestine,
whose destruction would likewise trouble no one. Strangely
enough, the demons name themselves "Legion" to Jesus, "for
we are many" (5:9).[22]

None of these explanations entirely succeeds, however, in
making sense of Mark's theology, and we are left confronting a
rather alien worldview, in which demons inhabit living beings,
whether human or beast, with devastating consequences. For
Mark, the real point is neither the willful destruction of animals
by Jesus nor political rebellion against the Romans. Rather, it
points to the hugely destructive power that these forces of evil

can wield over all life. Mark takes seriously these evil powers and, in this story, highlights their potential to cause havoc and Jesus' unique authority over them.

THE TEMPTATION STORY

Throughout the exorcisms, Mark's Jesus is portrayed as the "stronger" one (see 1:7; 3:27), the one who overcomes the forces of evil in whatever form they take, whether human or demonic, personal or political. Behind them lies the temptation narrative, which makes sense of all the exorcisms, revealing the intent of God's reign to overpower evil:

> And the Spirit immediately drove him out into the wilderness. He was in the wilderness forty days, tempted [or tested] by Satan; and he was with the wild beasts; and the angels waited on him [or ministered to him]. (1:12–13)

Mark's version of the temptation story is very short, much shorter than Matthew's or Luke's versions, and it is easy to miss. Occurring in the prologue to the Gospel (1:1–15), it sets the scene for what will follow, particularly in the exorcisms. In one sense, the Temptation is more a tableau than a story, couched in mythological language—that is, in cosmic language and imagery that make sense of what is occurring on the level of the historical and the everyday.

Immediately following his baptism, Jesus enters the wilderness, a place in the Old Testament associated with loneliness, hunger, want, trial, difficulty, and danger. There the one who is declared from heaven to be the "Beloved Son" (1:11) confronts the ultimate power of evil, Satan, for a period of forty days, a biblical number that parallels the years of the Israelites' wandering in the desert (Deut 29:5) or the days of the flood (Gen 7:12) or the period Moses spends on Mt. Sinai before the giving of the Law (Exod 24:18; 34:28).

Note that Mark says nothing of any actual "temptations" nor does he offer any clue as to what exactly Jesus confronts or how he does so. Instead, we hear only of the three beings who accompany him: first "the Satan" who "puts him to the test," then the wild animals, and finally the angels who "ministered to him" (*diakoneô*, 1:13). He is surrounded, in other words, by evil and by good: by the spirit who would tear him down (Satan), and by the spirits (the angels) who seek to build him up and nourish him.

In the middle of this tableau are the wild beasts, possibly symbols of lurking danger, but more likely symbols of harmony that stand on the side of Jesus with the ministering angels. The phrase "and he was" occurs twice, the first in relation to the desert and Satan, and the second in relation to the animals and the angels, suggesting two groupings, the last two joined together with Jesus: "*and he was* in the wilderness…being tempted by Satan; *and he was* with the wild beasts and the angels waited on him."[23]

There may be no explicit victory here, as in Matthew's and Luke's accounts, but it is surely implied in this picture of Jesus at peace with the wild beasts of the desert, unharmed by them[24] —like Adam and Eve at the beginning of creation (Gen 2:18–25) or Daniel in the lions' den (Dan 6:10–24). The Old Testament variously describes lions and wolves in the desert, leopards and foxes, hyenas and reptiles, wild donkeys and wild goats, ravens and owls, ostriches and antelopes, hares, badgers, and bears. Indeed, Isaiah unfolds a vision of wild creatures dwelling in harmony with domestic animals and humankind (Isa 11:6–7). This universal concord, beyond all the forces of evil and destruction, is achieved in this brief vision: the Markan Jesus, dwelling in harmony with the wild beasts and being ministered to by angels. Far from overpowering Jesus, Satan, the divider and bringer of discord, is hereby resisted and his baleful influence banished.

This is the symbolism lying behind the Markan exorcisms, the divine intent to restore creation in the face of the divisive and destructive powers of Satan and to enable all created things, both physical and spiritual, to inhabit together the one realm of God's good creation. In order to recreate that unity, all the forces that would corrupt, destroy, harm, and separate must first be overcome. Jesus, the Stronger One, is alone able to harness the celestial powers to make such consonance possible. The purpose of the kingdom of God that Jesus proclaims in word and deed is to clear the world of all its sin, violence, and disharmony in order to make way for God's peace and concord.

JESUS' IDENTITY IN MARK

In the Markan schema, so strongly influenced by Jewish apocalyptic thinking, Jesus' identity is key. It is often rightly remarked that the Jesus of this Gospel is presented as very human. He is reluctant to enter the desert and has to be "driven" by the Spirit (1:12). Later, he is reluctant to take the cup of suffering and prays in anguish for it to be taken from him, struggling with his own message of the kingdom (14:32–36). And he dies with a sense of having been abandoned by his God (15:34).

Yet this undeniable humanity—this creaturely fragility and vulnerability—needs to be set alongside Jesus' celestial identity, an identity made plain in two of the greatest moments of epiphany in Mark's Gospel, the baptism and transfiguration (1:9–11; 9:2–8). Jesus is first acclaimed as the Beloved Son beside the river, a divinely confirmed identity, as he is baptized alongside many others. The same heavenly affirmation is reiterated on the mount of transfiguration, where Jesus is surrounded by the uncreated light of heaven while conversing with two of its citizens (9:3–4). Ironically, this same identity, acclaimed at the beginning and in the middle of the Gospel, is proclaimed by the Roman centurion after Jesus' very human suffering and death by crucifixion (15:39). The celestial and the terrestrial merge together on the cross.[25]

At Jesus' baptism, Mark gives no immediate explanation for why the Son of God might require a "baptism of repentance for the forgiveness of sins" (1:4). Not until the sons of Zebedee attempt to make a deal with Jesus for power and prestige in the coming kingdom does Jesus reveal that the "baptism" is one of suffering and identification with sin: "Jesus said to them, 'You do not know what you are asking. Are you able to drink the cup that I drink, or be baptized with the baptism that I am baptized with?'" (10:38). As a human being, Jesus descends into the waters of sin and suffering in order finally to quench them. Only the

Beloved Son can achieve this, because only he possesses both the divine commissioning and the human solidarity that will enable him to do so.

JESUS' SUFFERING IN MARK

The cross is the place where Mark's theological perspective on suffering becomes most apparent. Mark prepares his readers carefully for this remarkable anticlimax. Everything leads up to it. Not for a moment are we in any real doubt about how the story will end. The theme of misunderstanding, rejection, animosity, and the resultant suffering marches hand-in-hand with the liberating mercy and power of Jesus' ministry. By the end of the first narrative cycle (2:1—3:6), an unholy alliance of Jesus' enemies is already plotting his death: "The Pharisees went out and immediately conspired with the Herodians against him, how to destroy him" (3:6).

In a real sense, Jesus' miracles push attention away from himself. He is no wonder-worker in this Gospel, seeking publicity and fame. There are times in Mark when Jesus explicitly forbids the disseminating of his powerful deeds and commands people to secrecy (e.g., 1:26, 8:26). Far from courting publicity, the Markan Jesus avoids it and retires into privacy again and again, either alone or with his disciples (e.g., 1:35). Indeed, it is not his power that will ultimately identify him but the very opposite— his renouncing of the power to save his own life for the sake of others: "He saved others; he cannot save himself" (15:31).

All through the journey to Jerusalem (8:22—10:52), Jesus announces his impending suffering, rejection, death, and resurrection to the utter bafflement of his followers. The journey narrative is carefully structured by Mark. Three times, evenly spread along the journey, Jesus unveils for his disciples the true mystery of his identity: that the Stronger One is also the Suffering and Crucified One. The third of these announcements is the most detailed:

> See, we are going up to Jerusalem, and the Son of Man
> will be handed over to the chief priests and the scribes,

and they will condemn him to death; then they will
hand him over to the Gentiles; they will mock him, and
spit upon him, and flog him, and kill him; and after
three days he will rise again. (10:33–34)

Each announcement is followed immediately by an incident that illustrates the bewilderment and incomprehension of
the disciples. After the first prediction, Peter tries to turn Jesus
from the path of suffering (8:32–33), a response that Jesus sharply
denounces, teaching instead the way of the cross as the way of
discipleship (8:33–9:1). Further along the way, after the second
prediction, the disciples quarrel among themselves about who
is the greatest (9:33–37), and Jesus responds by placing a child
in their midst, teaching them that acceptance and love for the
vulnerable and powerless are the true tests of greatness. Finally,
after the third prediction, the apostles James and John (who have
witnessed the transfiguration) ask for positions of power in the
coming reign of God (10:35–40), a response that infuriates the
other ten (10:41). The incident leads Jesus to outline, by contrast, the radical servant nature of true leadership as against the
power-hungry pursuit of domination and status (10:42–45).

One other explicit reference to Jesus' suffering and death
occurs immediately following the transfiguration, as the three
disciples descend the mountain with Jesus. In a discussion on
the role of Elijah who has just appeared and spoken to Jesus on
the mountain top, Jesus compares his own experience to that of
Elijah and continues: "How then is it written [in Scripture] about
the Son of Man, that he is to go through many sufferings and
be treated with contempt?" (9:12).[26] Clearly, the Markan Jesus
is thinking here of John the Baptist as an Elijah figure, expected
to appear at the end-time (1:2). Once again, the glorified Jesus is
identified with the one who suffers and is rejected rejected.[27]

Quite apart from what the passion predictions reveal about
Jesus' closest disciples and the paucity of their understanding,
they also enable him to expound the meaning and significance
of his own suffering. He is the one who takes the sorrowful path,
the path of self-denial. He is to be found not among the great
but among the least, among children and the like. He is the one
whose life and death embody servanthood. His death itself is an

act of voluntary bondage and servitude that paradoxically liberates those who are enslaved—a "ransom for many" (10:45).[28]

The shape of Jesus' ministry thus alters considerably with his change of direction after Caesarea Philippi and the transfiguration (9:2–13). Now the focus is on suffering and death, and what the image of the cross implies for discipleship. Here Mark shows a nuanced understanding of suffering. The rich man who approaches Jesus with a sense of emptiness and loss, despite his wealth and moral plenitude, is told not just to renounce that wealth but also to share it with those who are poor (10:17–22). Leadership means humble service for the good of others, renunciation for their empowerment, not lordly behavior and domineering structures of power for self-service (10:42–45).

In each case, the Markan Jesus shows an acute awareness of suffering and summons his disciples to alleviate and eliminate suffering wherever and whenever they can. The suffering of those who are poor, disabled, demon-possessed, and socially outcast, according to Mark, is not in any sense a good in itself, but rather something to be overcome through the power of prayer and the liberating impulse of God's reign (9:29). This theme has been clear throughout the Gospel.

Jesus thus calls disciples to embrace suffering—not to become poor for the sake of poverty, as if it were in itself a virtue, but in order to identify with those who suffer, in order to empower them and set them free. Leaders, in particular, are called to this kind of political "poverty," in which they renounce power even to the point of martyrdom, the ultimate act of self-giving, self-denying love for the sake of others. Their role is to act as servants for those in their charge, even as Christ has come as the Servant of all.

JESUS' DEATH AND RESURRECTION

Above all, Jesus himself willingly, if agonizingly, embraces suffering and does so in order to draw freedom out of suffering and life out of death. This is not a path he takes without painful struggle, as Gethsemane makes plain (14:32–42). His own sense of servanthood is part of the meaning of the cross for Mark. Indeed, the victory of the cross in Mark is deeply and disturbingly paradoxical. Jesus' death illustrates the point. In renouncing the power over his own life, the Markan Jesus surrenders everything, even his sense of the omnipresence of God. He dies with the loss of awareness of God's sustaining presence: "My God, my God, why have you forsaken me?" (15:34). In order to identify with the abandoned, he himself experiences abandonment; in order to identify with criminals, he experiences the punishment for sedition; in order to identify with the suffering, he himself suffers.

There is all the difference in the world, however, between the heart-rending manner of Jesus' death and a sense of despair and hopelessness: "The despairing person retreats into silence, whereas Jesus speaks. Although his speech is anguished and confrontational, it is still a kind of prayer and still a cry for help and support."[29] Mark indicates this in several ways. In the first place, the spirituality of the psalms allows for the expression of abandonment by God; indeed, it allows for all kinds of "negative" emotions that we might well consider beyond the spiritual pale. Jesus is quoting here a psalm of lament (Ps 22:1), in which the righteous sufferer expresses a profound sense of being abandoned by God to suffering, a sense that will lead him or her to a deeper apprehension of God's saving presence.[30] Jesus has not lost faith; his cry of dejection is addressed precisely to the God of his heart from whom he feels a painful distance: "Though he had heard no answer to his prayer, Jesus' prayer was heard after all; though he experienced abandonment and the absence of God, Jesus had not been forsaken."[31]

The Markan Jesus, in other words, stands in the biblical tradition of righteous sufferers, like Naomi, whose husband and children die in their prime and leave her alone (Ruth 1:19–21) or Job, who is deprived of everything for Satan's sport (Job 1:13–22) or the Servant in Isaiah, who suffers innocently on behalf of the people (Isa 53:3–5). Mark emphasizes this point in the passion narrative by showing the charges against Jesus to be trumped up and based on absurd and contradictory evidence (14:55–59) and by Pilate's obvious conviction of Jesus' innocence (15:6–15). Jesus is, par excellence, the righteous sufferer of the biblical tradition.

21

Furthermore, the centurion experiences a miracle of faith and perceives in this death Jesus' true identity. Where there is only the experience of divine absence for Jesus, the centurion discerns a divine presence: "truly this man was God's Son" (15:39).[32] The only human being in this Gospel to acclaim Jesus in these terms—and a violent and brutal Gentile outsider at that—the centurion suddenly perceives the cross as redolent with the presence of God, a God who descends into the depths of human dereliction, suffering, and pain.

Third, the apocalyptic signs surrounding the cross—the three-hour darkness before Jesus' death (15:33) and the tearing of the temple veil immediately following it (15:38)—underline for the reader/hearer the presence and the triumph of God in this otherwise seemingly godless event. Both are, in part, symbols of judgment against the religious and secular authorities who have crucified the Beloved Son, and against the old order of things. But both also possess positive symbolic meaning. The darkness invokes the solidarity of creation itself with Jesus' suffering, and the tearing of the temple veil dramatically opens the innermost presence of God to all, indicating a new creation.[33] For Mark, the cross, with all its terrible suffering, is nonetheless a cosmic event that fundamentally shifts the destiny of the world, suffusing it with divine presence, victory, hope, and meaning.

The final and most significant element of Mark's story, however, is the emptiness of the tomb and the angelic message of the resurrection on Easter morning. Jesus has already indicated his resurrection to his disciples on the road to Jerusalem as part of the passion predictions but, like the message of the cross, it has fallen on deaf ears. Or, to change the metaphor in terms of the two healing stories framing the journey to Jerusalem (8:22–26, 10:46–52), the eyes of the disciples have failed to perceive the message of the Gospel until a miracle of faith will restore their sight. Once again, with paradoxical intent, the absence of the body in the tomb is redolent of a profounder and deeper presence, beyond all powers of evil, sin, suffering, and death.

Jesus thus possesses a dual and paradoxical identity in Mark's Gospel in the cross and the resurrection, both possessing redemptive significance. On the one hand, he is the Servant of all, the Suffering and Crucified One, the Son of Man whose life and power are given over to others, freely and entirely, in his ministry and in his death on the cross. Faith and awareness of one's need is the only requirement for receiving the salvation offered by God's reign in this divinely given life and death.

On the other hand, Jesus is also the future glorious Son of Man who will return victorious at the end-time to render judgment on the earth, vindicating the people of God and putting an end to evil (13:26–27). This power over evil and all the forces of destruction is preempted in the ministry of Jesus in the exorcisms, in the transfiguration with its unearthly light and its implicit conquest of death, and above all, in the story and the message of the empty tomb, narrated by one of the citizens of heaven, which promises Christ's risen appearance in Galilee and his final appearance at the *Parousia*, the second coming.

INTERROGATING MARK

This overview of the way evil and suffering play out in the narrative of Mark's Gospel reveals what we may and may not demand of this text. As we have noted, Mark nowhere explains the problem of evil or the enigma of suffering. Instead, he gives emphasis to both in order to reveal the unmasking of the one and the promised elimination of the other. He includes within it the equally problematical nature of sin and death. On that basis, we can see what light Mark's Gospel might shed on the problem of suffering and death. How seriously does the Gospel take evil and sin in the world? How are suffering, sin, death, and evil overcome in this Gospel?

We have already seen that Mark has a good deal to say about suffering and evil, and that he takes both with the utmost seriousness. Indeed, the coming reign of God, already knocking at the door, deals precisely with the overthrow of evil and the eradication of suffering in their various guises and disguises. Mark sees this as an ultimate event. The signs of the kingdom are symbols that make real in the present moment the future reign of God. They are real in themselves but they are also promises of a future world remade.

But what difference does reading Mark make to our present experiences of suffering and evil? How does it affect our experience of sin, suffering, and death, and the sin, suffering, and death of the world?

In the first place, it assures us that these realities, though they seem dominant and all-pervasive, are not in any sense permanent but rather temporary and temporal. They are not part of God's full and final will for our lives, for our world, for creation. Their reality is far from being an ultimate one, even though it may feel so. God's vision for the future, for our future, is a very different one, and God's triumph is assured through the story of Jesus.

That assurance makes all the difference to our lives in the present moment. It is not simply a pious hope—a utopian dream— that is as far away as the proverbial rainbow's end. Indeed, it is not primarily our future at all, but God's, and God's future always impinges on the present, and is always breaking into it, just as Jesus breaks into history at the beginning of Mark's Gospel with his proclamation of the nearness of God's reign and the summons to an ongoing conversion of heart and life (1:14–15).

As we read the Markan Gospel and enter into the narrative with heart and mind and imagination, we are drawn further and further into the dynamic of God's reign. In touching the characters of the Gospel, we feel its fingers extending beyond to the text to make contact with us and our lives. We enter into the tale of Jesus' life and ministry and into the dynamics of his extraordinary death and resurrection. We reach the place where sin, suffering, evil, and death are definitively and ultimately dealt with. We are both spectators and participants in the drama at the place where sin is overcome by Jesus' sinless self-offering—where he is numbered with the transgressors (Isa 53:12)—where he dies a painful and humiliating criminal's death among convicts and scoffers.

We stand at a distance, with the holy women, looking on as the weight of human suffering is lifted from the world in Jesus' experience of dereliction and divine absence. At one level, we are observers at a death, a wake, a funeral, but at a deeper level, Mark shows us, to our astonishment, that we are gazing at the death of death, the death of our death, the death of creation's death. We are seeing with our own eyes the washing away of sin,

24

the ransom for the liberation of slaves and slavery, the infusing of triumphant joy and love into the deepest, darkest abyss of the world's suffering and anguish.

We are gazing, in other words, on the removal of sin and the atonement for innocent suffering. Jesus' death is a sacrifice for sin, as the Christian Tradition universally declares. The one without sin or guilt dies for the sinful and guilty, taking on and taking away their sin and cleansing them from guilt. This is a death for sinful human beings, but it is also the innocent one suffering for the innocent. He, the righteous sufferer of the biblical Tradition, suffers on behalf of all who have suffered without cause—all who have been deprived of freedom, love, understanding, and justice; all who have suffered pain, illness, and untimely death; all who have been tortured and martyred for righteous causes; and all who have done no wrong to warrant such suffering.

As human beings, we belong in both categories: we are both sinful and sinned against, we cause suffering and we receive it, we do wrong and we are wronged. Jesus' death, in Mark's Gospel, embraces us all, just and unjust, innocent and guilty, sufferers and sadists, lovers and haters. It is a death that also embraces the suffering of creation—a death that atones for everything and for all.

And all this takes place from within—even though the irony of the narrative seems to tell the very opposite. We are here in the blackest night at the very point where the dawn breaks, at the point of transition, where death gives way to life, suffering to joy, sin to freedom, evil to goodness. Fundamental to this transfiguration is the identity of the one who suffers. Only he can achieve this because he is the one on whom God's favor uniquely rests. Evil is overthrown from within by Jesus' succumbing to its malevolent power and allowing all its waves and billows to roll over him (Ps 42:7). He transforms it in that invisible moment, that momentous instant in time, through his divine goodness, his human innocence: from wickedness to righteousness, from death to life.

Only the Beloved Son can achieve the victory by this means, a victory-in-defeat, a transformation, the dredging of the cup of suffering until there is nothing left, no poison in the dregs, no bitter aftertaste. In this event, and through this unique person, fully human and fully divine, as the later Church expressed it, God rings out a final and definitive no to sin, evil, suffering, and death. God declares their reign to be over, and the reign of life, love, freedom, joy, and goodness to have begun. In reading Mark's Gospel, we have witnessed the turning of the ages and God's overcoming of evil:

> If it is from Christ that we are to learn how God relates himself to sin, suffering, evil, and death, it would seem that he provides us little evidence of anything other than a regal, relentless, and miraculous enmity: sin he forgives, suffering he heals, evil he casts out, and death he conquers. And absolutely nowhere does Christ act as if any of these things are part of the eternal work or purposes of God.[34]

True, that kingdom is not fully realized in our lives just yet, but it has begun, and begun definitively without possibility of turning back. The Strong Man of Jesus' parable has been over-powered, his house and belongings plundered and he himself is now a captive (3:27). Yet he is overpowered in a paradoxical way, not by triumph of war or greatness of might but by the even greater power of love and empathy, self-denial and identifica-tion, a power-in-weakness that only God can display.

How do we make contact with this hope, this paradoxical power in our lives, so often dominated by sin and death, by evil and suffering? The Gospel itself is the key, as we have already noted. If we participate in the Markan narrative, we too can be reached by its transforming power and grace. We can allow the future—God's future—to reach back into the present moment and embrace us with the arms of love and hope.

More than that, through the text of the Gospel and its sym-bolic working out in the life of the community of faith, we make contact with the one who has made contact with us, the one who has shared our suffering and taken upon himself our sin, who has identified himself with our innocent and unjustified suffer-ing, who has lived our life and died our death, who has subjected himself to the very worst that evil could muster against him. In knowing him, we come to know the God who has been made one with us, who has identified with our pain and anguish. We enter into a relationship with the suffering and crucified One, finding in that suffering and death the healing of our wounds, the death of our death, the source of our life and joy.

We too are called to enter into suffering and, in doing so for the sake of others, we enter into Christ's suffering, abandonment, and death, which is God's way of salvation. Suffering is part of our story, our mission, but it is suffering always suffused with hope and joy: "We, too, who all have a drop of suffering in our mission, should know that the Christian life flows into joy. It is no less bitter because of this hope, but it never gives birth to despair."[35]

Mark's Gospel gives no explanation for the existence of suffering and evil, nor does it inform us how a benign deity could permit such things to mar God's good creation. But the Gospel does demonstrate how God in Christ has taken on our suffering and evil, not abandoning us to our fate, but sharing it and transforming it from within. This is a past event and a future event, but in both cases it enters into our present moment, because the Son of Man who died and the Son of Man who will return is already going ahead of us into Galilee (14:28; 16:7). He is already with us, appearing from our past and from God's future, offering us healing, entering into our suffering, and walking with us into the valley of the shadow of death and from thence into the endless life of God.

TWO STORIES OF SUFFERING

If we are to look for relatively recent narratives that display something of Mark's emphasis on suffering and evil in human life and Christian discipleship, the instinct is to turn first toward instances of martyrdom where the Church is under persecution and has refused to give in to the powers of domination and idolatry. Certainly, such modern martyrs exist, their lives displaying confidence in the overthrow of evil and belief in the saving power of Jesus' suffering and death.

In South Africa, a girl named Manche Masemola came from a very poor family of the Pedi tribe in the Transvaal. Born around

1913, she became a Christian at the age of fifteen or sixteen, against the expressed wishes of her family. Over the next year, she attended the local Anglican mission in Marishane, run by Fr. Augustine Moeka of the Anglican Community of the Resurrection, intent on the study of the Bible and preparation for baptism. Her parents violently opposed her. She was forbidden to attend the mission or practice her Christian faith. Manche disobeyed her parents and continued attending church despite the harsh punishments she received.[36] One day Manche ran into the bush to hide from her parents' rage, but they found her and killed her. She died without being baptized, as she herself had predicted. As in the early Church, her death was her baptism in blood.

There is, however, a sequel to this tragic tale of domestic violence and teenage martyrdom. Manche's fate became widely known and her grave a place of pilgrimage for South African Christians. Her story, which spread rapidly across the country, brought many to faith. The greatest irony is that, forty years later, Manche's own mother came to faith through the witness of her martyred daughter, found forgiveness, and was received into the Church. Manche's martyrdom is commemorated on February 4 in the South African Church, and a statue of her, above the west entrance to Westminster Abbey, was unveiled in 1998.

The other narrative of personal suffering in a Christian guise is very different but equally related to the suffering of Christ. It is the story of a priest who contracted a slow version of motor neuron disease that eventually killed him. This terrible disease attacks the nerves controlling the muscles, which degenerate and die, so that in the end, the sufferer cannot walk or move, swallow or breathe. Geoffrey King, SJ, contracted the disease while he was still active as a priest and theologian. He wrote a remarkable article in the secular press, giving the reasons why he would not choose the option of assisted suicide, unlike others in his condition. There he admits that he is fully cognizant of the effects of the disease and grieves for what is no longer possible in his life: the walks, the cafés, the art galleries, the ferry rides he loved. Nonetheless, he continues to see his life as a gift from God, aware of the new gifts he experiences every day: solidarity with others in similar suffering and the love of those who care for him.

King's response to his debilitating ailment is grounded in the cross, in the belief that, on account of the suffering of Christ, all suffering—including his own—"can be redemptive." He concludes with compassionate recognition of those who have responded very differently to the same illness. He speaks, not in condemnation of those who fight for the right to take their own lives, but rather as one "who wants to live life to the full, who has found some of that fullness on the unlikeliest of places, and who trusts the amazing grace that has brought me safe thus far to lead me on."[37] Here, suffering is linked intrinsically to that of Christ, and to the triumph of the resurrection, resulting in a radically different outlook on the experience of suffering.[38]

Both stories portray the advent of evil and death in the lives of those who are innocent, who do not deserve such suffering. And yet both point to the redemptive power of suffering and even death in such contexts, through identification with Christ's own passion and his triumph over evil. They illustrate the difference a faith perspective makes when suffering and pain come unexpectedly and frighteningly into our lives, a perspective that is dependent on the New Testament's theology of suffering and triumph. Faith in the cross of Christ, in the suffering of God, is what enables the enduring of suffering and its transfiguration into life and hope.

CONCLUSION

God's final answer to suffering lies both in God's own suffering and also God's promised triumph over suffering.[39] God's final answer to evil, therefore, is the evil that is heaped on the Beloved Son. God's final answer to sin and death is to enter into it: to bear it on our behalf, in Christ, enduring and redeeming it from within, setting us free of its curse, its guilt, its anguish, its seeming finality. When we suffer, when creation suffers, when nations suffer, we are not alone. God, in Christ, suffers with us. When sinners crave forgiveness, they are heard and forgiven freely and generously. When the dying long for life and pray for freedom from suffering, both life and freedom are given them in and beyond the grave, and they make their journey into shadows in the company of the Son of God who also died and whose grave remains empty. When those afflicted by evil and violence cry out to heaven in pain and despair, there is an answering cry from God's future, already reshaping the present: the promise of a judgment, a vindication, a triumph, a conclusive setting free for us and for all creation.

None of this is an answer to evil and suffering in the conventional sense. It will not convince by argument and it will not affect the militant atheism and the materialism of our age. Philosophy does not have the power to transform our suffering, even if it could explain the reasons for suffering by careful reasoning and logic. Its wrists are tied before the reality of evil and death. Though science and education can mitigate the effects, they cannot finally eliminate these stark realities, the boundaries of our created existence. Human knowledge can do much to ameliorate the suffering and can sharpen for us the questions, but in the end, before the reality of death, it can do little more than wring its hands in grief and frustration or shrug its shoulders in stoic resignation.

In one sense, Mark's theological narrative can do much less than such a humanistic answer (if one exists), but in a deeper sense, it does far more. It can link our hands with the divinely human One who has entered into our sin, our suffering, and our death, knowing them from within, and has assured us by word and deed of their demise; who draws us into the triumphant dynamic of God's final reign; and who continues in compassion to walk our paths of misery and despair beside us, offering us in his company the joy and hope of forgiveness, freedom, transfiguration, and life.

Notes

1. An example of this is Bart Ehrmann, who, leaving behind the fundamentalism of his youth, found liberal Christianity equally inadequate to explain the existence of suffering and now describes himself as agnostic (N.T. Wright, "Bart Ehrmann: How the Problem of Pain Ruined My Faith," http://www.beliefnet

.com/columnists/blogalogue/2008/04/why-suffering-is-gods
-problem.html).

2. For the text of the interview, see http://www.age-of-the
-sage.org/quotations/quotes/stephen_fry_irish_tv_interview
.htm. For the live interview, see https://www.youtube.com/
watch?v=-suvkwNYSQo.

3. C. S. Lewis, *The Problem of Pain* (New York: Macmillan,
1944), 12–14.

4. C. S. Lewis, *A Grief Observed* (London: Faber & Faber,
1961), 15.

5. At Luke 23:47, the Roman centurion declares Jesus to be
dikaios, which means "righteous" or "innocent."

6. With this expression, Paul "transforms a slave's tattoo
or brand into a metaphor of his sufferings on behalf of the gospel...reminding his hearers that he is a slave of Christ" (W.K.
Williams, *Galatians* [Nashville: Abingdon, 1997], 167).

7. David Bentley Hart, *The Doors of the Sea: Where Was God
in the Tsunami* (Grand Rapids: Eerdmans, 2005), e-book, loc. 571.

8. See, for example, Martin Hengel, *Saint Peter: The Underestimated Apostle* (Grand Rapids: Eerdmans, 2010), 36–48.

9. See, for example, Francis J. Moloney, *The Gospel of Mark:
A Commentary* (Peabody: Hendrickson, 2002), 11–16.

10. The internal issues revolve mainly around Mark's use
of Latin and knowledge of Aramaic, as well as his lack of geographical knowledge of Galilee.

11. Jesus' secrecy about his identity in Mark—the so-called
"messianic secret"—is particularly apparent in the first half of
the Gospel and is associated with the theology of the cross: "Only
in suffering does the Marcan Jesus manifest his messianic status
in the full sense" (Martin Hengel, *Studies in the Gospel of Mark*
[London: SCM, 1985], 42).

12. The text of Mark provides alternative endings, neither
part of the original Gospel. Some have argued for a lost ending,
though there is no evidence of it. Further on this, see Joel Marcus, *Mark 8–16. A New Translation with Introduction and Commentary* (New Haven: Yale University Press, 2009), 1088–96. The real
question is how to interpret the women disciples' fear and silence
at 16:8. Is it disobedience on their part? If so, Mark may be direct-
ing it at his readers who "stand at the brink of the incomplete

narrative in which all have failed...with a decision to make" (M. Eugene Boring, *Mark: A Commentary* [Louisville, KY: Westminster John Knox Press, 2006], 449). Alternatively, it is holy fear the women experience, a fear that makes sense of other passages in Mark's Gospel (6:50; 9:6) and is thus appropriate in the light of what they have experienced; see, for example, Adela Yarbro Collins, *Mark*, Hermeneia (Minneapolis: Augsburg Fortress, 2007), 797–801.

13. For an overview of what researchers are saying about Mark's Gospel on a variety of relevant issues, see William R. Telford, *Writing on the Gospel of Mark* (Blandford Forum: Deo Publishing, 2009).

14. The Gospels would have been recognized in their own time as biography (*bioi*, "lives"). See Richard A. Burridge, *What Are the Gospels? A Comparison with Graeco-Roman Biography* (Grand Rapids: Eerdmans, 2004), 236–47.

15. For an outline of Mark's plot, see Francis J. Moloney, "Writing a Narrative Commentary on the Gospel of Mark," in *Mark as Story: Retrospect and Prospect*, eds. Kelly Iverson and Christopher W. Skinner (Atlanta: SBL, 2011), 101–12.

16. For the consensus view that Mark is to be dated to the period just before or just after the Jewish War (AD 66–70), see Boring, *Mark*, 14–15.

17. On Jesus' actions and what they reveal about Mark's Christology, see Elizabeth S. Malbon, *Mark's Jesus: Characterization as Narrative Christology* (Waco: Baylor University, 2009), 21–55.

18. Further on purity rites in the ancient Jewish world, see Archie T. Wright, "Jewish Identity, Beliefs, and Practices," in *The World of the New Testament: Cultural, Social and Historical Contexts*, eds. Joel B. Green and Lee Martin McDonald (Grand Rapids: Baker, 2013), 318–21.

19. For Mark's pictures of the disciples, see Robert C. Tannehill, "The Disciples in Mark: The Function of a Narrative Role," in *The Interpretation of Mark*, ed. William R. Telford, 2nd ed. (Edinburgh: T&T Clark, 1995), 169–95.

20. The typical pattern of the miracle stories is outlined in Rudolf Bultmann, *History of the Synoptic Tradition* (Oxford: Blackwell, 1963), 318–31.

21. On Mark's apocalyptic worldview and the role of exorcisms within it, see Brendan Byrne, *A Costly Freedom: A Theological Reading of Mark's Gospel* (Collegeville, MN: Liturgical Press, 2008), 1–14.

22. See Joel Marcus, *Mark 1–8: A New Translation with Introduction and Commentary* (New York: Doubleday, 2002), 350–52. Marcus also points out the stupidity of the demons in unintentionally causing their self-destruction.

23. On this episode, see Boring, *Mark*, 46–48, who points out the ambiguity in the presence of the wild beasts.

24. See Mark Bredin, *The Ecology of the New Testament: Creation, Re-Creation, and the Environment* (Colorado Springs: Biblica Publishing, 2010), 41–46.

25. Dorothy A. Lee, *Transfiguration* (New York: Continuum, 2004), 9–37.

26. "Son of Man" is a difficult title in the Gospels. In Mark, it is used of Jesus' ministry, suffering, and future coming. It is probably an apocalyptic title (Dan 7:13) that now, for Mark, includes Jesus' ministry and suffering (Moloney, *Mark*, 212–13). For a summary of the debate, see Delbert Burkett, *The Son of Man Debate: A History and Evaluation* (Cambridge: Cambridge University Press, 1999).

27. Elijah is an important figure for Mark; the identification of John the Baptist as a figure in the tradition of Elijah is made on the basis of John's clothing (1:6; 2 Kgs 1:8).

28. As Boring points out, Mark is not specific about how exactly Jesus' death is saving, but leaves it open as a mystery (*Mark*, 302–3).

29. Collins, *Mark*, 755.

30. There is no need to assume that Jesus has in mind the whole of the psalm at this point, which ends on a note of praise. His suffering here, for Mark, is very real. See Morna D. Hooker, *The Gospel According to St. Mark* (London: A & C Black, 1991), 376.

31. Boring, *Mark*, 432.

32. The Greek can mean "a son of God" or "the son of God." Despite the ambiguity, for Mark this is an affirmation of Jesus as *the* Son of God (see 1:1, 11; 3:11; 5:7; 9:7; 14:61–62). See Camille Focant, *The Gospel According to Mark: A Commentary* (Eugene: Pickwick, 2012), 644–45.

33. Timothy C. Gray, *The Temple in the Gospel of Mark: A Study in Its Narrative Role* (Grand Rapids: Baker Academic, 2008), 185–94.

34. Hart, *The Doors of the Sea*, loc. 727.

35. Adrianne von Speyr, *Mark: Meditations for a Community* (San Francisco: Ignatius Press, 2012), 375.

36. See Rebecca St. James, *Sister Freaks: Stories of Women Who Gave Up Everything for God* (New York: Alive Communications, 2005), Week 5.1. On the statue of Manche, see the Westminster Abbey site, http://www.westminster-abbey.org/our-history/people/manche-masemola.

37. Fr. Geoffrey King, SJ, "Life or Death Decision Inspired by Faith in God," *The Age*, April 4, 2013.

38. A young man in a similar position to King, and with similar faith, writes, "We do not seek pain for its own sake, but our suffering can have great meaning if we try to join it to the Passion of Christ and offer it for the conversion or intentions of others. While often terrifying, the suffering and pain that we will all experience in our lives can be turned into something positive" (Phillip G. Johnson, "Dear Brittany: Our Lives are Worth Living, Even with Brain Cancer," The Catholic Diocese of Raleigh, http://www.dioceseofraleigh.org/content/raleigh-seminarian-terminal-brain-cancer-responds-brittany-maynard).

39. The Eastern Orthodox Church generally does not accept the view that God suffers on the cross; only the humanity of Jesus actually suffers since God is beyond all suffering (see Hart, *Doors of the Sea*, loc. 626–51). There is, however, a way of understanding how God in Christ enters into human suffering, not to be overwhelmed or altered by it, but in order to identify with it in radical love and overcome it; see, for example, Gary Culpepper, "'One Suffering in Two Natures': An Analogical Inquiry into Divine and Human Suffering," in *Divine Impassibility and the Mystery of Human Suffering*, eds. James F. Keating and Thomas J. White (Grand Rapids: Eerdmans, 2009), 77–98.

Chapter 2

_____

FEAR AND ANXIETY AND THE GOSPEL OF MATTHEW

CONTEXT

Fear and anxiety are widespread problems in our world. We live in a time when most people's lives are affected by fear at one time or another, while others live their whole lives in its shadow. Beneath the daily fears is the sheer uncertainty of all our living—because we never gain the assured stability, in this life, that we crave.

Fear is not an unnatural experience; animals also feel it. Indeed, it may be reasonable for us to be afraid in the presence of danger, and threats to our security and well-being may be well-grounded. Poverty, unemployment, domestic and other forms of violence, ill health, and tragedy are real possibilities for most people. The inevitability of death gives rise to deeper levels of fear. Given the transience of our lives and the suddenness with which disaster can strike, it is not surprising that we fear or that our lives are filled with anxiety. Indeed, we need to take fear seriously; we have every right to make provision for future possibilities and eventualities, even when we know they cannot do more than delay the inevitability of death.

Fear can also manifest itself collectively and culturally: in threats to national security, violence, and terrorism. Again, this fear may be natural in many contexts. But it can also be manipulated through various media in our society to create what has been called "a culture of fear." The term originated in 1997 with the sociologist Frank Furedi, who has subsequently continued his warnings against the fearmongering of our culture, so that it has "become a cultural idiom through which we signal a sense of growing unease about our place in the world."[1]

This fear culture magnifies the presence and possibilities of terrifying scenarios, whether in the home or in society at large, with alarmist theories that intensify the normal sense of human anxiety well beyond the actual dangers present. Insurance companies do a roaring trade on such fears, encouraging us to shore up our lives against the future. The consequences of the "fear-floating character of our fear narratives," are a paralyzing avoidance of risk-taking and an exaggerated stress on safety, the glorification of powerlessness, and the difficulty in creating trust: "fear itself becomes the problem."[2] Indeed, we can become afraid of fear itself.[3]

Fear and anxiety are not necessarily identical, though they overlap. Fear has a discernible object that can be understood and confronted. It presents as a more dramatic and mercurial emotion, often immediate, although it can also suggest a fixed refusal or inability to face a specific situation or context. Anxiety, by contrast, is generally long-term and can be chronic, less dramatic in presentation perhaps, and based on deeper levels of unhappiness that are persistent. Moreover, an existential kind of anxiety (associated with death and the lack of meaning) need have no defined object.[4] It can be a recurrent sense of dread or foreboding that has no specific focus. Both fear and anxiety demonstrate their presence in bodily symptoms.[5]

Anxiety is perhaps the most difficult of all emotions. Passion, anger, rage, and hatred can be understood and channeled, but anxiety is different. It may have no simple solution, especially if the roots are deep and complex. Psychologists know about anxiety because they have to deal on a daily basis with those who are afflicted with anxiety disorders, often associated with depression. Even without mental illness, however, people experience anxiety: about their own health and that of their families and relationships, about loneliness and isolation, about wealth and security, about unemployment and disability.

Whether fear or anxiety, our lives cannot and should not be haunted by them. We do not need to live perpetually in their shade. People should not have to live in places where their homes and families are continually under threat of violence, where they are forced to flee in terror, sometimes meeting not with hospitable asylum but with suspicion, imprisonment, and rejection. Nor should we have to live with anxiety dogging our steps at every turn, our hearts and minds dominated by fear, day and night. There is a freedom from such debilitating fear—a freedom too from nagging, everyday anxieties that we yearn to find and that so few of us possess.

FEAR IN THE OLD TESTAMENT

The Bible has a good deal to say on the subject of fear. In biblical narratives, fear is something that motivates people to act and respond in certain ways. Jacob is motivated by a fear of his brother's justifiable rage after he steals Esau's birthright (Gen 27:41–45); he is similarly motivated when he sends his family and servants across the Jabok years later before his meeting with his brother (Gen 32). Moses flees Egypt in fear after he kills the Egyptian who is beating a fellow Israelite (Exod 2:11–15). Saul's jealous fear of David leads him to murderous rages so that in the end David is forced to go into hiding (1 Sam 19). The Apostle Paul, soon after his conversion, attempts to join believers in Jerusalem but they are afraid of him, and he has to prove his credentials before they accept him (Acts 9:26–28). The merchants and traders of Babylon stand in fear as they watch and lament the oppressive city's downfall (Rev 18:9–10).

Oddly enough, one of the most striking and perhaps (to our minds) disturbing things the Bible has to say on the subject is that the fear of God is a good and beneficial thing. The fear of the Lord is said to be the beginning of wisdom (Ps 111:10; Prov 9:10; Job 28:28) and knowledge (Prov 1:7), and again and again, the same fear is invoked as the basis of the authentic life of faith.

Both testaments attest to the importance of this theme; indeed, it is intrinsic to Judeo-Christian spirituality. The wisdom writings, in particular, speak of the fear of God in the most astonishing terms. Not only is it associated with wisdom and knowledge, it is also linked to hatred of evil (Prov 8:13), longevity (Prov 10:27), confidence, refuge, and life (Prov 14:26–27, 19:23).[6]

It is clear from these assumptions about the benefits of living in this way that we are not speaking here primarily of fear as the abject terror of God's disapproval and wrath—although for those who practice idolatry and injustice, such a response is not entirely out of place (e.g., Isa 3:13–15; Amos 1:3—2:8). The Bible maintains a place for God's judgment and wrath against all that distorts and corrupts, all that demeans and injures. More often, however, the fear of God signifies the awe we feel in the presence of God, an awe that is intended, not to alienate, but rather to draw us closer, to lead us to deeper levels of trust in and love of God.

In the theological sense, human beings ought to fear God for the simple reason that God is God, utterly different from us, entirely other to us, transcendent mystery, self-contained, and without need of us. We fear God because God is the radiant perfection of love, beauty, and justice, way beyond our imaginings. We fear God because, in that divine holiness, our best efforts at goodness and integrity seem threadbare, and our pettiness and inability to love stand out in comparison. We fear God because, in God's merciful presence, we come face-to-face with our own fierce longings, our most painful thirst, our restless striving. Such aspects of God are indeed terrifying.

This kind of fear, however, is very different from the natural fear of disasters, or the fear of other people's responses to us, or fear of misfortune and tragedy. They stand almost at opposite ends of the spectrum. The one—the fear of God—is life-giving and creative, drawing us deeper and deeper into the path of wisdom and awareness, freedom and life, as we move toward the sublime mystery and love that is God. The other fear, when it overtakes us, is crippling and paralyzing, deathly, pushing us into a dark corner where we lie cowering and trapped. Indeed, we could say that the authentic "fear" of God is the antidote for all the other kinds of fear that are so harmful to, and ensnaring of, our lives.

WHY THE GOSPEL OF MATTHEW?

So why choose Matthew, of all the Gospels, to explore the theme of fear and anxiety? The other Gospels also address this subject. Indeed, Matthew's most famous passage on anxiety in the Sermon on the Mount (Matt 6:25–34) has a direct parallel in the Gospel of Luke (Luke 12:22–31), though the context is different. Nonetheless, it is possible to argue that Matthew does give our theme a greater emphasis than the other evangelists, not just in the number of times fear-language appears, but in other emphases, as we will see, that bear on the question of fear.

When we read Matthew's Gospel (on any theme), we find ourselves in dialogue inevitably with the Gospels of both Mark and Luke. It is more than likely that Mark's was the original Gospel, the first to be written, as we have already noted,[7] and that both Luke and Matthew followed Mark's basic outline and many of his stories and characters. The fact that the Gospel of John has a different outline for Jesus' ministry and different stories, and even, in some cases, characters, makes this point clear. None of the Gospels is attempting a literal, chronological account of Jesus' own ministry, but each is shaping the events of Jesus' life and death with a theological purpose in view.

To read Matthew aright, therefore, involves taking seriously the use he has made of Mark—the changes he has made, the omissions and the expansions; these latter are significant, amounting to twelve additional chapters. It also involves glancing over the back fence, as it were, to Luke's Gospel, which is involved in a similar process of editing Mark.[8] If Matthew is, indeed, using Mark and writing in a later period, it is likely that his Gospel was written sometime after the end of the Jewish War (AD 66–70). It is less likely—though not impossible—that the apostle Matthew was the author (9:9; 10:3); Matthew was, and remains, a common enough name, and our author may well have been a Christian scribe (13:52).[9]

Perhaps the most noteworthy point about Matthew's changes to Mark's structure is the addition of teaching material. These teachings are gathered into five discourses throughout Jesus' ministry: the Sermon on the Mount (5:1—7:17); the Mission Discourse (10:1–42); the Parables (13:1–53); the Community Discourse (18:1–35); and the Apocalyptic Discourse (24:1—25:46). These alternate with accounts of Jesus' actions—mostly miracles—and the controversies with the authorities whom he engages. Matthew stresses Jesus as Teacher,[10] a teaching that is drawn from the Old Testament—largely the wisdom and apocalyptic traditions within Judaism.

We read Matthew, therefore, as a storyteller and theologian in his right, placed first in the canon of the New Testament not necessarily because of his priority in time, but more likely because of his strong and positive emphasis on the life of the Church and its teaching. As we will see, for example, Matthew tends to tone down the harsh and somewhat negative treatment the disciples, who embody the Church, receive in the Gospel of Mark.

Matthew is also the most Jewish of all the Gospels, though it also betrays the signs of recent separation from the Jewish synagogue.[11] It represents a form of Jewish Christianity that, while open to the Gentiles, emphasizes the ongoing relevance of the Law of Moses for discipleship. Jesus becomes the definitive interpreter of the Law, which he lives out in authenticity of life in both word and deed. He is in one sense a new Moses, giving the Law, but in another and deeper sense, he transcends Moses because of his unique identity as the Son of God.[12]

Unlike the previous chapter, where we examined the problem of suffering and evil, we are not dealing here with a major philosophical dilemma. As we have already noted, fear has a number of causes: biological, psychological, social, cultural, and political, and while these are of concern to the Gospel writers, they are also attempting to reach the religious and spiritual issues that underlie the others. Given also that we are reading Matthew, the great teacher of the Law, we will need to ask about any moral and ethical implications that fear might have on our lives.

So our questions for Matthew are somewhat simpler than the ones we addressed to Mark, though every bit as profound. Is it possible to live without an overwhelming and paralyzing sense of fear and anxiety? If so, how can we achieve such free-dom? What words of wisdom, insight, and comfort might this Gospel have to offer to enable the healing and liberating of anx-ious souls?

EXAMPLES OF FEAR IN MATTHEW

Before we answer these questions directly, we need to gain some sense of Matthew's understanding of fear and the narra-tive contexts in which he addresses it. There are a number of instances of fear in Matthew's story, and it takes different forms and expresses different emotions, some more comprehensible than others.

In the infancy narratives, for example, Joseph makes a deci-sion based on fear (2:22). He has been guided in his protective care of mother and child by his dreams and the angelic voices that speak to him. Forced to flee from Herod the Great's paranoid fury and living in exile in Egypt, Joseph wants to return to his own land with his family but is afraid of returning to Judea, given that the ruler is Archelaus, one of Herod's sons.[13] Instead, Joseph moves to Galilee. As it transpires, Joseph's fear is well-founded and his action in avoiding Judea an eminently sensible one.[14]

A rather different fear is shown by the Jerusalem authori-ties who want to arrest Jesus much later in the gospel narrative (21:46). They need to do so by stealth and deceit because of Jesus' popularity and their fear of public opinion. Like that of Joseph, this fear is both political and well-founded, but in other respects, the two fears are very different: the one fears for the safety of a vulnerable child, the Son of God; the other represents fear for political and social standing, as an act of judicial murder is con-templated.

A similar fear of public opinion is present in the story of the beheading of John the Baptist. Now it is Herod Antipas who wants to put John to death for his fearless outspoken criticism of Antipas's lifestyle but is afraid of the Baptist's popularity (14:5; cf. 21:26). In each case, the Jerusalem authorities and Herod Antipas find ways around their justifiable fear, and succeed in putting to death the prophetic figure who has dared to challenge and confront their hypocritical and oppressive behavior. Their fear does not inhibit them from committing an act of gross injustice.[15]

A rather different kind of fear is found in the parable of the talents, which is one of three parables in Matthew's Apocalyptic Discourse (25:14–30). The factor that prevents the third slave from making use of his talent, leading him to bury it—unlike the other two who are most enterprising—is, he claims, the fear of his master that, rather than motivating him, has an enervating effect on him (25:25). The consequence is rejection by his master for laziness and timidity. For Matthew, the parable is given an apocalyptic twist that goes beyond the moral details of the scenario.[16] Now it is a case of final judgment and the way disciples have used their spiritual gifts in the cause of the kingdom of heaven.[17] The story of the third slave is an example of the fear that paralyzes.

The soldiers at the crucifixion are also afraid following the apocalyptic events that surround the cross, and particularly the earthquake (27:54). In Mark's account, the response of the centurion is a confession of faith, but in Matthew, the words are uttered not just by the centurion but also by the other soldiers and suggest a more ambiguous meaning. These are the same people who have dressed up, mocked, struck, and abused Jesus, forced an innocent bystander to carry the crossbeam, offered Jesus mockingly a drink of bitter wine, crucified him, divided his remaining possessions, placed the title on the cross, and sat down to keep watch (27:27–37). The soldiers' responses to the three-hour darkness, the tearing of the temple veil, and the earthquake come from sheer terror in Matthew's account rather than faith. The sublime identity of Jesus that they have mocked and abused, they are now compelled to acknowledge on account of the supernatural events that have occurred. Their reaction—though the words they utter are true—is drawn from dread: fear for their own safety and terror of the unknown representing all that lies beyond their grasp.

The same group at the tomb manifests a similar fear when they experience the earthquake and appearance of the angel rolling back the stone (28:4). This is the only account in the Gospels where nonbelievers encounter something of the resurrection. And it is unclear when exactly Jesus himself emerges from the tomb. These guards who, in the passion story are "the actual actors of evil rather than Pilate,"[18] now faint with a kind of numinous dread at the terrifying presence, luminosity, and strength of the angel—just as they have reacted to the apocalyptic signs of the crucifixion, with a confession drawn reluctantly from their lips.

For the Roman soldiers, this is not a life-giving event. On the contrary, soon after, they will allow themselves to be bribed into propagating a lie, a lie that undermines their own competence to keep guard—that the disciples stole the body while they slept (28:11–15). This fear in the presence of the heavenly has no lasting effect on the soldiers; they are impervious to what they have seen, both at the cross and at the tomb. Perhaps the lie they tell makes it easier for them to deal with their own terrifying experiences.

FEAR AND FAITH

The characters who most often experience fear in Matthew's Gospel, however, are the disciples.[19] Joseph is afraid of marrying Mary, not comprehending the source of her pregnancy until it is revealed to him (1:18–20). The disciples are afraid of the rising, cataclysmic storm on the Lake of Galilee (8:25). They will also, by implication, be afraid of those who persecute them (10:26). Generally, this kind of fear indicates an inadequate degree of faith on the disciples' part. The phrase "you of little faith" (which is a single adjective in Greek, *oligopistos*) occurs five times in Matthew's Gospel in relation to the disciples (6:30; 8:26; 14:31; 16:8; 17:20). Though softening Mark's portrait of the disciples' lack of understanding, Matthew demonstrates that, on each occasion, the disciples' fear outweighs in the balance their faith. Elsewhere, Matthew's Jesus asserts that only a small amount of faith is needed, the size of a grain of mustard seed, in order to move mountains (17:20).

A prime example of this kind of fear—which also serves an important metaphorical function in teaching about discipleship—is Simon Peter's request to walk on the water with Jesus (14:22–33). Peter's desire springs from a remarkable level of faith, courage, and daring. He climbs out of the boat confidently enough, but fear overtakes him at the first tug of the stormy wind and he begins to sink, crying out in terror, his courage and faith deserting him (14:30). The lesson, for Matthew, is that fear has the capacity to take the focus away from the majestic figure of Jesus to the menacing dangers surrounding us. Even here, however, Jesus' hand stretches out at once to save the frightened disciple, drowning in fear and panic.

There is the other kind of fear too, the dread associated with the celestial identity of Jesus in this Gospel, apparent in his moments of epiphany: in his walking on the stormy seas at night before the disciples (14:26); in his luminous presence on the mountain at the transfiguration before Peter, James, and John (17:6); and in his living presence at the tomb to the women disciples (28:1–8). This fear at the tomb is, for Matthew, in no sense paralyzing. It is explicitly linked to joy: leaving the tomb, they ran with "fear and great joy" (28:8). It is a numinous fear but one that is overtaken by joy, which is not identical to the women's previous fear of the angel. There it was the unknown; now, through the angel's message, it is the known and the loved, and it is filled with obedient faith.

It is worth noting here that Matthew unambiguously clarifies the indistinctness of the women disciples' response at the end of Mark's Gospel: "And they said nothing to anyone, for they were afraid" (Mark 16:8).[20] Matthew's modification of the references to the women's fear, the changing of "fled" to "ran," and the omission of reference to the women's silence, not to mention their encounter with the risen Christ himself, all make clear that the fear they experience finally is a holy fear, based on faith and obedience.[21]

Several times throughout the Gospel, the Matthean Jesus issues calming instructions in the face of the disciples' fear: "Do not be afraid" or "do not fear." Joseph is told in a dream not to fear to marry Mary because of the divine origins of her pregnancy (1:20); he at once obeys and follows the angelic directions. Jesus asks the disciples why they are afraid on the raging waters before turning to rebuke the storm, implying that in his company, they need have no fear (8:26). In the Mission Discourse, the disciples are promised that they will have no need for fear or anxiety, either about the words they will have to speak when they are put on trial (10:19) or about their persecutors in general. These may have the power to hurt the body but cannot touch the life of the soul, which is kept safe and intact through the disciples' faith (10:26, 28).

When it comes to otherworldly fears, Jesus is equally reassuring. When they are afraid of ghosts, Jesus soothes the disciples' fear with his flesh-and-blood presence (14:27). On the mountain, when they hear the divine, celestial voice confirming Jesus as the Beloved Son—exactly the same words used at the baptism (3:17)—their dread is calmed by Jesus' approach and touch. The words, "Do not be afraid" (17:7) are words of consolation at the presence of an epiphany.[22] Similarly, the angel utters the reassuring words to the two women disciples at the tomb on Easter morning—"Do not be afraid" (28:5)—giving them, in place of their fear, the astonishing news of the resurrection and the commission to proclaim the joyful message.

There is thus a kind of fear that is perhaps close to what we might call "awe" or "reverence" that is entirely comprehensible, emphasizing the gulf that yawns between the celestial and terrestrial realms. Comfort may be needed so that this fear does not paralyze or unduly terrify, but it is essentially the fear of holiness and otherness that is a natural and appropriate response to the proximity of the divine.

On another level, there is one fear that Jesus does advocate, and that is the fear of Satan: the one who can "destroy both soul and body in hell [*Gehenna*]" (10:28). It is only what causes lasting and irreparable damage that is to be feared. There is nothing numinous about this fear; it is the dread of being finally rejected from the kingdom of heaven, the fear of missing out on that which is of most value, that which possesses all beauty and goodness. It is also the fear of evil itself, evil at its source, because of its capacity for sheer, mindless destruction; for its propensity to undo the good and create endless havoc, irreparable harm. These are things to be feared—and especially by those who are indifferent to the moral code of the kingdom, and its concern for uprightness of heart and integrity of life. Leaders who practice hypocrisy and injustice are most in danger of this profound loss and ought most to fear it (cf. 23:1–36).

ANXIETY IN THE SERMON ON THE MOUNT

Matthew speaks not only of fear in general but also, more specifically, of worry and anxiety. Perhaps the best-known passage on the subject is the section on anxiety found in the Sermon on the Mount:

> Therefore I tell you, do not worry [*be anxious*] about your life, what you will eat or what you will drink, or about your body, what you will wear. Is not life more than food, and the body more than clothing? Look at the birds of the air; they neither sow nor reap nor gather into barns, and yet your heavenly Father feeds them. Are you not of more value than they? And can any of you by worrying add a single hour to your span of life? And why do you worry about clothing? Consider the lilies of the field, how they grow; they neither toil nor spin, yet I tell you, even Solomon in all his glory was not clothed like one of these. But if God so clothes the grass of the field, which is alive today and tomorrow is thrown into the oven, will he not much more clothe you—you of little faith? Therefore do not worry, saying, "What will we eat?" or "What will we drink?" or "What will we wear?" For it is the Gentiles who strive for all these things; and indeed your heavenly Father knows that you need all these things. But strive first for the kingdom of God and his righteousness, and all these things will be given to you as well.
>
> So do not worry about tomorrow, for tomorrow will bring worries of its own. Today's trouble is enough for today. (6:25–34)

The Sermon is very carefully structured, beginning with the Beatitudes (5:2–10) and ending with the parable of the two foundations (7:24–27). Chapter 6 contains at its heart—and at the center of the Sermon, itself—the Lord's Prayer.[23] Its theme sets out the three classic religious duties of pious Jews who wish to follow the path of "righteousness": almsgiving (giving to the poor, 6:1–4), prayer (6:5–15), and fasting (6:16–18). It is not just a matter of fulfilling these sacred obligations, Matthew declares, but also of performing them in the right spirit.

From this perspective, Matthew's Jesus moves on to speak positively, first, about treasure and wealth (6:19–24) that are to be found in heaven rather than on earth and, second, against anxiety, particularly for the basic necessities of life: food and clothing. These two subjects, treasure and anxiety, are linked by the theme of one's heart being in the right place. The anxiety passage begins with the words "Therefore...," indicating that it is a continuation of the discussion on treasure and wealth.

The passage on anxiety is organized in a symmetrical pattern or ring structure, where different parts of the discourse correspond to each other:[24]

A. Do not be anxious about food & clothing (6:25)
  Reason: life & the body are worth more than food & clothes
  B. Birds: fed by God (6:26)
    Disciples of more value
    C. Anxiety cannot change anything (6:27)
  B.1 Wildflowers: clothed by God (6:28–30)
    Solomon not as beautiful
    God will clothe disciples
A.1 Do not be anxious about food & clothing (6:31–34)
  Reason: God knows disciples' needs
  Alternative focus: the kingdom
  Summary (v. 34): Do not be anxious for tomorrow

The emphatic repetition of "do not worry" at the beginning and the end of the passage sets the pattern of encouragement offered: disciples are commanded not to be anxious about where their food and drink and their clothing are to come from. This is an extension on the discussion concerning treasure. Because their "treasure" is in heaven, disciples are not to be concerned to shore up their lives against material want or to pursue material needs obsessively. Their dependence is to be on God. In the center of the pattern is the statement that anxiety makes no difference, in any case. The final proverb about worrying only for today provides a summary of the whole passage, again with the emphasis being on disciples' material needs.

The passage stands in the wisdom tradition of the Old Testament, which speaks of "the bread of anxious toil" (Ps 127:2) and declares that anxiety "weighs down the human heart" (Prov 12:25) and "brings on premature old age" (Sir 30:24). Anxiety is to be banished from the good life, a life lived before God (Eccl 11:10), and worry over wealth is particularly futile, depriving one of sleep (Sir 31:1). Indeed, personified Wisdom herself, among her many divine qualities of goodness and beneficence, is also entirely "free from anxiety" (Wis 7:23). Here, as elsewhere in the Gospel, Matthew's Jesus is drawing on ancient wisdom traditions within Israel that view anxiety as inimical to the life of the wise.[25]

All the same, the passage is not particularly easy to interpret. It uses the language of command rather than encouragement. It seems to imply that work is an unnecessary burden, and that disciples should live without it. It appears to suggest that sparrows never starve and that flowers always grow, portraying an idyllic world without famine or drought,[26] though Matthew's emphasis on the healing miracles of Jesus indicates that he has no such rosy vision of the world. Nonetheless, the imagery does advocate a radical life for discipleship that cuts to the very heart of an accommodating Christianity where the accumulation of wealth, insurance policies, and long working hours are presupposed and even commended. In raising these objections, Ulrich Luz argues for a realistic interpretation of the text that is prepared to ask the question of "what significance poverty, the forgoing of vocation, or renunciation of work could have in the service of the kingdom of God."[27]

Within this framework, Matthew's Jesus gives four reasons why disciples can, and should, live their lives without anxiety. In the first place, anxiety is unnecessary, since God already knows the material needs of his disciples and will provide them with food and clothing. It is a waste of time and effort to worry about food and clothing, given God's prior knowledge and awareness of the lives and needs of disciples. In the same way, in the Lord's Prayer, disciples are encouraged to pray, "Give us this day our daily bread [bread for the coming day]" (6:11).[28]

Second, anxiety goes against the pattern of nature itself, where God shows provision for all the creatures of the earth, including the plants. In order to underline the point, Matthew's Jesus uses two examples from nature: the birds of the air that do not need to work hard for their food, and the wildflowers that make no effort but whose clothing is splendid and beautiful. Both examples illustrate the providential mercy and care that God shows to his creation. Trust in that goodness is dependent on knowing who God is and what God is like, and believing that God will provide for the needs of disciples. Disciples are of greater value than birds or wildflowers and will thus, even more, be provided for as Jesus says elsewhere: "You are of more value than many sparrows" (10:31).[29]

Third, anxiety about material possessions is a distraction. There are more important things in human life than what we are to eat or what we are to wear. Note that Jesus does not say that only spiritual things matter and that the body is unimportant. He says here that there are more important things for the *body* than its clothing: its health and wellbeing, for example. In Matthew's Gospel, Jesus shows a clear concern for people's physical wholeness, as many of the miracles make plain. For the disciples, in particular, such worry is a real barrier since their focus needs to remain fixed on bringing to earth the kingdom of heaven and promoting everywhere the righteousness of God.[30]

Lastly, anxiety evinces a lack of faith and trust in the providential goodness and kindness of God. Twice in this passage, God is referred to as "your heavenly Father" (6:26, 32), which is the appropriate designation for disciples calling upon God in the Lord's Prayer: "Our Father in heaven" (6:9). It expresses both the transcendent mystery of God ("heavenly," "in heaven") and also the intimacy of God's parental love and care ("Father"). Throughout Matthew's Gospel, the title *Father* is used of God more than forty times and more than two-thirds of these occur in the Sermon on the Mount.

Thus, for Matthew, anxiety among disciples represents a serious challenge to the nature and goodness of God. In the Sermon on the Mount, Jesus presents an image of God whose main characteristic is an overflowing grace, forgiveness, and goodness to all and sundry. The good and the evil are equally the recipients of sunshine and rain, which God sends indiscriminately on all (5:45). In the sixth of the antitheses—statements where Matthew's Jesus presents his interpretation of the Law over against previous teaching—the theme is love of the enemy, as against older traditions that have commended love for friends and permitted hatred of the enemy. Disciples, by contrast, are called to show the same indiscriminate love demonstrated by God, not just to friends and lovers but also to enemies and haters (5:43–48).

If disciples are to be truly centered on God and on the kingdom of heaven, moreover, they should neither be wedded to wealth nor should their lives be consumed by constant worry, "a paralyzing anxiety that can only enervate discipleship."[31] The disciples who live out the "better righteousness"—that excess of goodness and integrity that following Jesus and his interpretation of the Law implies (5:17–20)—need to ensure that their hearts are right, as well as their actions. If they are indeed "pure in heart" (5:8) in their commitment to God's reign, truly dedicated, then they will live their lives without the presence of crushing and chronic anxiety.

It is this quality in God, this divine indiscriminate goodness, that liberates disciples from daily anxiety. God's merciful providence and care for his creation are to be trusted. As Jesus says elsewhere, even the sparrow is cared for by God who observes the death of each one; how much more therefore are disciples valued by God (10:31)? Indeed the opposite of anxiety, for Matthew, is trust—trust in the providential goodness and kindness of God.

To live without anxiety, therefore, for Matthew means to live in perfect trust and faith in the generosity and forgiving grace of God. To be anxious implies the lack of such trust and a paucity of faith in the very nature of God, the God revealed in Jesus. What is at stake here is the question of who God is. As with the instructions on prayer, Matthew emphasizes that God does not need to be bribed or manipulated in order to hear and respond to the needs of supplicants. God already sees, already knows, and already provides (6:7–8).

Furthermore, as we have noted, anxiety for Matthew distracts disciples from the center and heart of their vocation. They are called to live for God's reign, to practice and promote the radical values of the kingdom of heaven, to "hunger and thirst" for that kingdom (5:6), and to do everything in their power to enable it to become a reality in human life. Anxiety muffles that commitment and that calling, drawing disciples away from their deepest passion, their truest mission. God's providential care for the disciples frees them to work toward the dawning of a new day where, in the imagery of the Lord's Prayer, the earth will be as filled with the holiness, sovereign rule, and will of God as is heaven itself (6:9–10); the one will mirror perfectly the other.

ANXIETY AND DIVINE PRESENCE

There is a further element in Matthew's call to disciples to live a life without anxiety. This element goes beyond the Sermon on the Mount to the beginning and end of Matthew's Gospel. The birth and infancy stories are tied to God's purpose, expressed either in the agency of Joseph's dreams or in the five Old Testament quotations that are scattered throughout the story. The first of these explicitly names Jesus as "Emmanuel" and Matthew gives the translation: "God is with us" (1:22–23); Jesus' coming signifies the divine presence dwelling with people. The same motif closes the Gospel. The last words of the risen Jesus to his disciples on the mountain in Galilee are "And remember, I am with you always, to the end of the age" (28:20). The first and last divine words of the Gospel—the Old Testament and the risen Christ—attest to Jesus' abiding presence with his disciples, with his Church, with humankind, with creation, guaranteeing through that presence the attendance and companionship of God.[32]

The Gospel miracle that captures the theme of divine presence is the storm at sea with the disciples in the boat (8:23–27). We have already taken note of this story and its challenge to the disciples' fear. However, it is significant that, unlike in Mark's version of the story (Mark 4:35–41), Matthew has Jesus first rebuking the disciples in the very midst of the storm and only then calming it (8:26). Once again, the theme here is Jesus' presence, even in a situation of menace and danger; disciples need not fear, not just because Jesus will calm the storm, but rather more fundamentally because Jesus is with them.[33] He shows no anxiety and is able to sleep peacefully. Disciples are called to the same freedom from anxiety because of Jesus' presence with them and, through him, God's presence. This is the ultimate reason for the directive to disciples not to be anxious. It is not because storms will be kept at bay or because they will be kept unharmed—on the contrary, persecution and trouble are inevitable—but because God in Christ is intimately present to them, with them, and among them, a God who cares and who knows and who ultimately provides.

INTERROGATING MATTHEW

Having grasped something of the complexity of how Matthew presents fear and anxiety throughout the Gospel, as we interrogate it, we bring the questions of our culture to an ancient text that does not interpret human behavior in modern, psychological, or sociological terms. Whatever answers the Gospel text provides, these do not rule out our own insights and knowledge to help us understand ourselves and find ways to live without perpetual fear and anxiety.

The questions with which we began centered on the issue of whether or not it was possible to live without fear and anxiety and, if so, how that might be achieved. We asked whether Matthew might have words of comfort and wisdom for us and for our society to enable us to move beyond fear. As we have explored something of Matthew's perspective, we already know that the answer to our questions is neither simple nor straightforward.

Matthew has a good deal to say to us: not just to his own community or the early Church but to our very different world today. He teaches us what to fear—evil in its every guise—and what not to fear because of God's saving presence—persecution, trouble, uncertainty, danger. He shows us the beauty and splendor of God in Jesus Christ, through epiphanies on the mountain, on the waters, at the tomb, and the awe that can transform our lives. He opens for us a world where we can be free of anxiety, free to have faith in the beneficence of our Creator who loves and knows each one of us, providing for our needs with the bounty of the earth—each person, each animal, each plant. He draws us into trust and knowledge, into intimacy and presence, into hope and promise of the future reign of heaven already challenging and changing our present, little by little, piece by piece, like a tiny mustard seed planted in the garden that finally grows, through patience and nurture, into a tree that shelters the wild birds (13:31 32).

Matthew weaves the problem of fear through the themes of his narrative: in his understanding of the nature of God and Christian spirituality, in his presentation of the identity of Jesus Christ and the purpose of his coming, in his focus on the Church's life and mission, in his apocalyptic message, and in his focus on the Law and ethical living. Through epiphany, healing, teaching, dying, and rising, the Matthean Jesus offers a new way of living without fear, even in risk and danger; and without anxiety, even in the uncertainty of material possessions. His answer to fear and anxiety is based on a clear spirituality, grounded in the nature of God as revealed in Jesus' birth, life, ministry, death, and resurrection.

There is thus the possibility of a life lived without fear or anxiety. It becomes a real prospect for those who will learn the lesson and the wisdom of trust, who will take hold of the God of Jesus and entrust themselves and their lives entirely to that God. Matthew's theology undergirds his spirituality of what is, in one sense, an authentically carefree life, where disciples become centered on the things (the "cares") that really matter: the kingdom or reign of God and God's righteousness. Being centered in this way leads disciples more deeply into the realms of faith and further away from the imprisonment of fear and anxiety.

ANXIETY AND MEDITATION

Having set out something of Matthew's theological perspective on the reality of fear and anxiety, and its pertinence to our context, it is worth asking a further question at this point: How can we access this spirituality in our own lives? The fact is that telling people they ought not to be afraid or anxious can lead in the opposite direction, that of increased anxiety and a loss of self-worth at the perceived failure to trust the gospel message. It is true that what Jesus is doing in Matthew in response to the disciples' fear is a form of loving encouragement rather than a bleak command. The Matthean Jesus calls his disciples to live more and more out of the generous-hearted self-giving of God who is always and utterly to be trusted.

One method of dealing particularly with personal anxiety is silence and meditation. The practice of mindfulness, often associated with Buddhism, is of special value in dealing with everyday anxiety. Mindfulness is a disciplined method of meditation in silence and stillness, in which the meditator gently and consistently distances him- or herself from all thoughts and feelings, observing them instead in a noncritical and nonjudgmental way. Studies in psychology have confirmed the usefulness of mindfulness in lowering anxiety. One study demonstrates not only its assistance in dealing with anxiety, but also the parts of the brain changed by such practice. Defining *anxiety* as "the inability to control emotional responses to perceived threats," the clinical trial studied the brain scans of fifteen people before and after mindfulness training, and noted the significant reduction in activity in certain parts of the brain.[34]

This, and similar studies, are based on a secular view of mindfulness that is similar to, but not identical with, Christian understandings of meditation. Christian faith has a strong tradition of silence and stillness in prayer, with a focus on awareness that is very similar to mindfulness. Nonetheless, it is open to drawing on secular learnings and insights from other faiths. These insights concern not so much the content of meditation but rather the method, the "how" of meditating. These techniques are simply ways of engaging Christian content and, for our purposes, the wisdom that Matthew's Gospel brings to bear on the problem of anxiety.[35]

In the Christian Tradition, there have been two impulses in meditation, which are different in style and approach but not necessarily in contradiction. The one, the "apophatic" (literally, "away from words"), is a form of contemplation based on "negative theology" that says that the best way to speak of God is by describing what God is not. In this form of prayer, the meditator seeks to move beyond all thoughts and feelings into the word-less presence of God. This style of meditation emphasizes the transcendence and mystery of God, beyond all ego, and is associated particularly with *The Cloud of Unknowing*,[36] St. John of the Cross (1542–91) and, more recently, Thomas Merton (1915–68). It is also the form of prayer developed by the monk John Main (1926–8?), which has developed since his death into the World Community of Christian Meditation.

The second form of meditation is the "kataphatic" (literally, "moving into words"), which is also based in stillness and silence, but uses images and imagination to find connection with God. It is not an intellectual exercise but rather one that engages the soul in the deepest place. It is associated particularly with St. Ignatius of Loyola (1491–1556) and often focuses on biblical narratives—especially from the Gospels—in which the meditator enters the story and engages at a deep level with the presence of Christ.

Both these styles of meditation, and their variants, employ mindfulness in their teachings on prayer. The basic tenet is that mindfulness is primarily associated with God; it is God who is, first and foremost, mindful of us and self-revealing in all forms of prayer and meditation. The style of prayer associated with John Main is, in one sense, a Christian form of mindfulness. It is based on the use of a mantra (Main suggests the Aramaic Mara-natha, the great Advent prayer meaning "O Lord, come"). The meditator focuses on the repetition of the mantra, the sacred word, whenever thoughts and feelings intrude. The purpose of this kind of prayer is not explicitly for relaxation or even the reduction of anxiety. It is nothing other than the presence of God and being entirely in the present moment, which, though it may not seem productive during the meditation, is ultimately transformative for the whole of life. It is not a matter of wrestling with anxiety but rather of resting in the transforming presence of God beyond our egos.

Ignatian meditation is similarly not directly focused on decreasing anxiety but rather on encountering God in a way that makes possible transformative decisions in our lives, contemplation in action. Self-awareness is the equivalent of mindfulness in this kind of spirituality, in which we become more and more aware of feelings and thoughts. Through imagination, we enter the Gospel stories and find healing through encounter with Christ in the narratives or other types of imaginative meditation.[37] Mindfulness, indeed, is present in the biblical writings, in their focus on recollection and recognition: remembering the past and God's action in creation and redemption, and recognizing in hope God's beneficent plan for the future.[38] One obvious aspect of mindfulness in Ignatian meditation is the Examen prayer at the end of the day, which involves a scanning of the day to discern the presence of God and express gratitude for that presence.

These forms of meditation are ways of learning trust in the God who is present in all things and to all things. They are not an immediate cure for anxiety—still less, a quick fix—but a significant by-product of their use of mindfulness is a substantial reduction in anxiety. Indeed, as we have noted, such meditation results in positive changes to the brain, leading to a deeper and broader sense of peace and well-being.[39] In Christian understanding, it reduces anxiety both through nonjudging self-awareness and also a deepening sense of divine love and presence in which our lives can rest. When Jesus speaks as Divine Wisdom, he is inviting disciples into a closer and more trusting union with God, which relieves us of the burdens that weigh on us, including anxiety:

> Come to me, all you that are weary and are carrying heavy burdens, and I will give you rest. Take my yoke upon you, and learn from me; for I am gentle and humble in heart, and you will find rest for your souls. For my yoke is easy, and my burden is light. (11:28–30)

The easy yoke of which Jesus speaks here is the yoke of the Law, as interpreted and lived out by Jesus himself. In the context of this discussion, it could be described as the discipline of meditation and mindfulness practice that may require effort to initiate and maintain, but which provides that Sabbath rest for the soul that frees us more and more from anxiety, drawing us into closer union with Christ and deeper trust in God's providential goodness.

INTERVIEWING MATTHEW

We might develop this discussion of Matthew on fear and anxiety in another way, which captures in summary the message of his Gospel for our contemporary context on this particular issue, through the use of imagination. Let us imagine for a moment that we have asked a modern journalist to interview St. Matthew on the subject of fear—perhaps part of a wider project on what ancient writers can contribute to our understanding of issues in contemporary life. We might call our journalist "Rebekah" and assume that she knows something of Jewish and Christian traditions. We might also assume that Rebekah has recorded this interview with Matthew and transcribed it for us.

Rebekah: Rabbi Matthew, thank you for agreeing to this interview on the subject of fear. As you know, it's part of a wider project I'm engaged in, looking at several writers from the ancient world and what, if anything, they might have to offer us today on this subject. I have already interviewed Cicero, Plutarch, and Philo of Alexandria, and now I'm exploring the theme of fear with you. I've read your Gospel book, of course, with considerable interest. And I'm very grateful that you've taken the time to speak to me.

Matthew: It's my pleasure, Rebekah. I'm clearly in exalted company with those you've already interviewed!

Rebekah: Well, at least your writings are much shorter than theirs! You have quite a bit to say on the subject of fear in your book. Let me begin by asking whether you see anything positive at all in fear. Mostly, you're quite negative about it. Is it something that has to be overcome in our lives?

Matthew: Not at all. On the contrary, I believe that fear is an important and even necessary aspect of our lives. There are things in our world that are, objectively, very frightening and we do well to fear them. The power of evil is such an example. I call this power "Satan" but your culture probably is uncomfortable with that notion. I notice in your newspapers a good deal about widespread threats of terrorism from extremist groups. Some of them call themselves religious, which I find hard to believe. No power that wants to harm others can come from God; the righteousness of heaven is always generous and merciful, loving all people and desiring their good—even the ones we fear and dislike. Those who want to harm and destroy in the name

57

of heaven have their motivation from Satan, from the powers of evil and not from God. And we need to protect those who are vulnerable to them.

Rebekah: What kind of "protection" do you have in mind here?

Matthew: It involves being prepared, as Jesus was, to speak out courageously against evil and expose the menace, the terror, for what it really is: not the voice of true religion but the ungodly ambition to gain power over the lives of other people. We also need to be prepared to stand up in support of those whose lives are most under threat. God has a special care for those who are vulnerable, the "little ones," as Jesus called them, the ones who are needy and unprotected. However, what it doesn't involve on our part is hatred—not even hatred of those who are most violent and destructive. We have to resist the temptation to fall into the trap of hating them just because we're afraid of them. We're called to pray for them, as much as to pray for the victims of their terror. Judgment, after all, is not in our hands. We need to fear hatred as much as we fear terrorism; both, after all, come from the same source, from Satan.

Rebekah: So the only real fear is the fear of the destructive forces, including hatred?

Matthew: Well, yes and no. There's another kind of fear that we also need: what the Bible calls the "fear of the Lord." It means partly the dread of God's judgment, which is a terrifying thing. Later generations than mine, I believe, came up with all kinds of distorted images of judgment: a kind of eternal torture chamber. That's certainly not what I was talking about. To me, the judgment of heaven happens in and through our rejection of God and God's goodness and justice. It's a kind of mutual antipathy, a mutual rejection, if you like, where God rejects those who have rejected God.

Rebekah: But doesn't that picture of God make your religion a frightening one?

Matthew: No, it doesn't, because judgment isn't the main point. God does not desire judgment, but the good and well-being of all people. The "fear of the Lord" really means a sense of awe in the presence of God, a sense of the awe-inspiring mystery and beauty of God.

Rebekah: How does that help—aren't we still speaking of a terrifying presence?

Matthew: No, awesome rather than terrifying. Sometimes people were so awestruck in the presence of Christ that they could hardly stand, like Peter, James, and John at the transfiguration or Mary Magdalene and the other Mary at the empty tomb. But they were reassured at once, their fears were calmed. God doesn't actually want us to live our lives in terror and anxiety—even of God!

Rebekah: In our society, Rabbi, people are generally very anxious. Anxiety is like a kind of disease—even devoutly religious people can suffer from chronic anxiety. What's your message for them?

Matthew: They need to recapture a sense of who God really is, the God who is revealed in Jesus. This is a loving God who is generous to everyone not just to Christians, but to all people. This is a God who cares not just about the spiritual and religious things, but also about the everyday reality of people's lives. God knows that we worry about money and about food and clothes and housing and all the other material things. God cares for the whole of creation, every creature under heaven. And God provides for us all.

Rebekah: Aren't you just giving people who have anxiety problems a lecture on how they should feel? What difference will saying such things make to their lives? Lectures make anxious people feel even worse about themselves—guilty as well as anxious.

Matthew: It's not meant to do that. It's true that anxiety and fear are not easily overcome. They can't be dismissed with a magic wand. It's natural for us to be afraid, and Jesus in his life, in my view, was both kind and forgiving to his disciples when they were frightened. He wanted them not to be afraid, but he understood their fears. You see, the opposite of anxiety is not security—we can never get that in this life—but trust. And trust is something we grow into, little by little: through prayer, through silence, through meditation. We come to trust in the goodness, the generosity, the mercy of God. And slowly but surely we become more trusting, so that the more we trust and the more we abandon ourselves to God, the less we fear, the less anxious we become. We need patience for this journey, and kindness toward ourselves as well as toward others. But trust comes in the end.

Rebekah: So where does your view of Christ come into all this? Does believing in Jesus make any difference to our fears?

Matthew: Yes it does, but it's not a quick fix. Jesus himself went through the most fearsome experience on the cross to save us, and he warned his followers that they would also suffer misunderstanding and abuse. We believe that Jesus will one day return to remake the world: a world without fear or injustice or evil of any kind. But, for now, Jesus is risen from the dead, he has escaped the clutches of fear and death and evil; he has overcome them, for us and for everyone. And he promises to be with us in all our experiences: in our fears and anxieties, in our struggles, in our striving for the kingdom. That's the great comfort we're given. And it is with that teaching that I ended my Gospel—with Christ's promise to remain with us till the end of time: through thick and thin, through joy and sorrow, through faith and fear.

Rebekah: Thank you very much, Rabbi Matthew. You've made your points very clearly. You really do have something to say worth hearing. It was good to meet you!

Matthew: Thank you, Rebekah. Shalom!

CONCLUSION

Matthew's Gospel portrays different kinds of fear and anxiety, some of which are more problematical than others. The sense of awe in the presence of God, and revealed in Christ himself, is something that is both natural and desirable, providing it does not overwhelm us. Other forms of fear are much more difficult and have no place in the life of discipleship. In this respect, Matthew has a significant contribution to make to those forms of fear and anxiety that cripple our lives and absorb too much of our attention, forming so dominating a part of our public and private lives. His answer, as we have seen, lies not in the building of vast and costly structures of security to protect us from the fearful things, the things that make us anxious. It lies rather in opening ourselves more fully and completely to a God who is at all times and in all ways to be trusted—the God communicated in Jesus' life and teaching on discipleship, his death and resurrection. Jesus' own experience in the desert is both an enabler and a model for us to follow. His capacity to live "by every word that comes from the mouth of God" (4:4; Deut 8:3) demonstrates the kind of trust that liberates us from anxiety. In this process, developing a practice of Christian meditation can assist us in touching the liberating grace of God and becoming more and more aware of ourselves in the light of God's acceptance and love.

Notes

1. Frank Furedi, *Culture of Fear Revisited: Risk-Taking and the Morality of Low Expectation* (London/New York: Continuum, 2006), vii

2. Ibid., 4, 175–99, 1–5.

3. Franklin D. Roosevelt is responsible in 1933 for the famous saying "The only thing we have to fear is fear itself" (first inaugural address as President of the United States, http://historymatters.gmu.edu/d/5057/).

4. Paul Tillich, *The Courage to Be* (London: Fontana, 1952), 44–48. Tillich identifies three types of anxiety: fate and death, meaninglessness, and guilt (48–61).

5. See, for example, Susan M. Orsillo and Lizabeth Roemer, *The Mindful Way through Anxiety* (New York: Guildford Press, 2011), 20–22.

6. See, for example, 2 Chr 19:9; Ps 34:11; Sir 4:26–27; Acts 9:31; 2 Cor 7:1; Phil 2:12; 1 Pet 2:7; and Rev 14:7.

7. See introduction, pp. xx–xxi.

8. On Matthew's use of Mark and the Sayings Source, he most likely shares with Luke (Q), see especially Warren Carter, *Matthew: Storyteller, Interpreter, Evangelist* (Peabody: Hendrickson 2008), 47–65.

9. For a summary of the introductory issues to Matthew, see W. D. Davies and Dale C. Allison, *Matthew: A Shorter Commentary* (London: T & T Clark, 2004), xi–xxix. For somewhat different conclusions, see Donald A. Hagner, *Matthew 1–13*, World Biblical Commentary, vol. 33a (Nashville: Thomas Nelson, 2000), xxxix–lxxvii.

10. See Paul S. Minear, *Matthew: The Teacher's Gospel* (London: Darton, Longman & Todd, 1982), who, in emphasizing this theme, speaks of the five discourses as five manuals of instruction on which the Matthean plot turns (1–23).

11. See Carter, *Matthew*, 66–91, for an outline of the likely context of Matthew's community in relation to the Jewish and Greco-Roman worlds.

12. On Matthew's use of Moses symbolism throughout the Gospel, see especially the study by Dale C. Allison, *The New Moses: A Matthean Typology* (Minneapolis: Fortress, 1993).

13. Archelaus (23 BC–c. AD 18), one of Herod the Great's sons, was a cruel ruler over the Roman-controlled region of Judea; Rome gave him the title of "ethnarch" rather than "king." At one point he ordered the massacre of three thousand Jewish protesters in the Temple. He was eventually deposed by the Romans in AD 6. The story is told by the Jewish first-century historian, Josephus in *The Jewish War* (Penguin Classics, 1981, Kindle edition), loc. 2076–2297 (Book II).

14. This account of how the Holy Family ends up in Galilee is in some tension with Luke's version, where Nazareth in Galilee is their original home and they move to Judea only for the census (Luke 2:1–5). On the differences between the two narratives, see Raymond E. Brown, *The Birth of the Messiah: A Commentary on the Infancy Narratives in Matthew and Luke* (New York: Doubleday, 1977), 32–37.

15. Herod Antipas (21 BC–AD 39) was the son of Herod the Great and brother of Archelaus; after his father's death, he became "tetrarch" of Galilee. John the Baptist disapproved of his taking the ex-wife of his brother, Philip, and was murdered by him; Jesus also refers to him as "that fox" (Mark 6:14–29; Luke 13:32).

16. See Brendan Byrne, *Lifting the Burden: Reading Matthew's Gospel in the Church Today* (Collegeville, MN: Liturgical Press, 2004), 189–92.

17. It may be that Matthew prefers "kingdom of heaven" to Mark's "kingdom of God" as a pious Jewish avoidance of the name *God*. Alternatively, it could illustrate Matthew's understanding that the "kingdom of heaven" will eventually replace all earthly kingdoms (see Jonathan T. Pennington, *Heaven and Earth in the Gospel of Matthew* [Leiden/Boston: Brill, 2007], esp. 279–330).

18. Ulrich Luz, *Matthew 21–28: A Commentary*, Hermeneia (Minneapolis: Fortress, 2005), 610.

19. For a study of the disciples in Matthew, their understanding and misunderstanding, especially from 16:21–20:28 where the focus is most intense on their narrative role, see Jean-

nine K. Brown, *The Disciples in Narrative Perspective: The Portrayal and Function of the Matthean Disciples* (Atlanta: SBL, 2002), 59–93.

20. It is not entirely clear in Mark whether the women disciples' fear is based on disobedience and thus the failure of all Jesus' disciples, male and female (e.g., Francis J. Moloney, *The Resurrection of the Messiah: A Narrative Commentary on the Resurrection Accounts in the Four Gospels* [New York: Paulist Press, 2013], 13–18) or holy awe and silence (Adela Yarbro Collins, *Mark: A Commentary*, Hermeneia [Minneapolis: Augsburg Fortress, 2007], 794–801). For the view that the original ending of Mark was lost and the Gospel unfinished, see R. T. France, *The Gospel of Mark: A Commentary on the Greek Text*, NIGNTC (Grand Rapids: Eerdmans, 2002, 670–88).

21. Moloney, *Resurrection*, 46–47.

22. On the nature of this kind of fear at the Transfiguration, see Dorothy Lee, *Transfiguration*, NCT (London: Continuum, 2004), 55–58.

23. See Ulrich Luz, *Matthew 1–7: A Commentary*, Hermeneia (Minneapolis: Fortress, 2007), 212. On the triadic structure of the Sermon, see W. D. Davies and Dale C. Allison, *A Critical and Exegetical Commentary on the Gospel According to Saint Matthew*, 2 vols. (Edinburgh: T&T Clark, 1988), 1:63–64.

24. This pattern is usually called a *chiasm*, because it works rather like the Greek letter "ch."

25. The most famous example is where Jesus himself speaks as Wisdom, summoning disciples to take on his easy yoke and promising them the gift of rest (Matt 11:28–30; see Sir 51:23–27). See Donald Senior, *Matthew*, ANTC (Nashville: Abingdon, 1998), 131–34.

26. Luz, *Matthew 1–7*, 402–3.

27. Ibid., 412.

28. Hagner, *Matthew 1–13*, 161.

29. The Bible mentions eagles, owls, sparrows, ravens, doves, falcons, swallows, kites, ostriches, hawks, cormorants, partridges, cranes, storks, pigeons, and quails. On God's provision of food for the ravens and their chicks, see Job 38:41.

30. For a summary of Matthew's view of righteousness, see Richard A. Burridge, *Four Gospels, One Jesus? A Symbolic Reading* (Grand Rapids, MI: Eerdmans, 2005), 82–83.

31. Hagner, *Matthew 1–13*, 163.

32. David D. Kupp sees Matthew as possessing an "Emmanuel Christology" and traces it throughout the gospel narrative (*Matthew's Emmanuel: Divine Presence and God's People in the First Gospel* [Cambridge: Cambridge University Press, 1996], 49–108).

33. See R. T. France, *The Gospel of Matthew*, NICNT (Grand Rapids: Eerdmans, 2007), 335–36.

34. Fadel Zeidan et al., "Neural Correlates of Mindfulness Meditation-Related Anxiety Relief," *Journal of Social Cognitive and Affective Neuroscience* (June 3, 2013): SCAN 1–9.

35. For suggested mindfulness techniques, see especially Orsill and Roemer, *The Mindful Way*, 95–121.

36. This is a book on contemplative prayer written in Middle English during the fourteenth century by an anonymous writer. See *The Cloud of Unknowing and Other Works* (Penguin Classics, 2001).

37. See, for example, the meditations in Anthony de Mello, *Sadhana, a Way to God: Christian Exercises in Eastern Form* (New York: Doubleday, 1978), which are based on a Christian form of mindfulness.

38. See Aloysius Pieris, "Spirituality as Mindfulness: Biblical and Buddhist Approaches," *Project Muse: Today's Research, Tomorrow's Inspiration*, https://muse.jhu.edu/article/381792.

39. See, for example, Rick Hanson, *Buddha's Brain: The Practical Neuroscience of Happiness, Love, and Wisdom* (Oakland, CA: New Harbinger Publications, 2009), esp. 79–96.

Chapter 3

THE QUEST FOR MEANING AND THE GOSPEL OF JOHN

CONTEXT

The question we are addressing to the Gospel of John is rather different from those of the previous two chapters. There we explored themes clearly present within the Gospel. Admittedly, we noted that Mark is not attempting to answer our questions; nonetheless suffering and evil are both explicit in Mark's Gospel, as is fear in the Gospel of Matthew. In taking the search for personal meaning and fulfillment to the Gospel of John, however, we are exploring a concept that does not explicitly appear in the Johannine narrative. So why ask the question at all of the Gospels (or the New Testament), and why address the question to John?

In a strange way, it is legitimate to ask questions of the Gospels that they themselves do not ask, provided we make due allowance for the limitations of the text. It may be that the questions will not be answered directly, or that they will be re-formed in the dialogue. But the original questions are not of themselves illegitimate. In any text considered "canonical" or even "classic," there is a sense that its voice can speak across generations, cultures, and worldviews—even more so with a religious text such as the Bible, and the accompanying belief of Christians that the Spirit who originally inspired its writings inspires also its interpretation in future generations. We can ask the question of meaning, therefore, and wait to see if and how the text might answer us.

In the well-known account of his three horrendous years in a Nazi concentration camp, the writer and psychiatrist Viktor Frankl discovered through painful experience the search for meaning to be "the primary motivational force" in human life.[1] As a Jewish prisoner living with constant deprivation at every level of his life and the daily threat of death, he noticed during his time that those fellow inmates who retained a sense of meaning tended to survive over those who did not: "Woe to him who saw no more sense in his life, no aim, no purpose, and therefore no point in carrying on."[2]

The pursuit of meaning lies at the heart of our life as human beings, whether we are conscious of it as a specific quest or not. The modern world interprets this as a deeply personal search, but in the ancient world—as in parts of the world today—meaning was something given within a culture, within a religious and mythological framework, within an extended family. In the post-Enlightenment culture, with the breakdown of traditional social structures and values, meaning has become an individual quest, with relatively fewer givens to enable a sense of self-understanding, life direction, or shared values. It is a much more haphazard and hazardous enterprise in the contemporary context, with an emphasis that previous generations could not, perhaps, conceive.

This is not to say that no meaning is to be found in ordinary lives. Most people find meaning in their work, their relationships, and their leisure, but whether that meaning of itself is enough to satisfy something deeper is another question. The quest for meaning is not simply the search for what gives a sense of satisfaction and enjoyment in the transience of the everyday—in friendship, family, and work—but in a sense of connection to something deeper and more abiding. C. S. Lewis called this deep desire the "inconsolable longing," a thirst for ultimate meaning and significance in and beyond the daily realities of our lives. He describes it, somewhat haltingly, in these terms:

> In speaking of this desire for our own far-off country,
> which we find in ourselves even now, I feel a certain

shyness. I am almost committing an indecency. I am trying to rip open the inconsolable secret in each one of you—the secret which hurts so much that you take your revenge on it by calling it names like Nostalgia and Romanticism and Adolescence; the secret also which pierces with such sweetness that when, in very intimate conversation, the mention of it becomes imminent, we grow awkward and affect to laugh at ourselves; the secret we cannot hide and cannot tell, though we desire to do both....The books or the music in which we thought the beauty was located will betray us if we trust to them; it was not *in* them, it only came *through* them, and what came through them was longing. [These things—the beauty, the memory of our own past]—are good images of what we really desire; but if they are mistaken for the thing itself they turn into dumb idols, breaking the hearts of their worshippers. For they are not the thing itself; they are only the scent of a flower we have not found, the echo of a tune we have not heard, news from a country we have never yet visited.[3]

C. S. Lewis is by no means the first to speak of this longing. It belongs within the mystical tradition of the Church and has a long and venerable history. Perhaps the most famous depiction of this longing for God comes from St. Augustine: "You have made us and drawn us to yourself, and our heart is unquiet until it rests in you."[4] It is this restlessness, this "spirit of divine discontent and longing," that lies at the heart of the search for meaning.[5] It is a profoundly spiritual quest that crosses religious boundaries, a "timeless yearning for union with something beyond ourselves" that lies in the depths of the human heart and that no earthly thing can satisfy.[6]

This longing is a desire to be overtaken, even consumed by the holy mystery of a transcendent reality. Goethe's poem, "Holy Longing" (*Selige Sehnsucht*), captures this well. He uses the image of a butterfly fluttering toward a lighted candle and being consumed by desire for the flame:

Distance does not make you falter.
Now, arriving in magic, flying,
and finally, insane for the light,
you are the butterfly and you are gone.

The poem is in praise of "what is truly alive, / what longs to be burned to death,"[7] presenting the paradox of life and death, "death" here being metaphorical for the sense of being ecstatically at one with a reality that is beyond and yet that is also the ground of our every existence. This union is a kind of destruction of the ego, though it is the source of life for the true self.

The current context demonstrates that the meaning to be found in the everyday is not always or adequately life-giving: always there remains a longing within and beyond. Christian understandings of meaning, embedded in the biblical heritage, address not only the question of where meaning is to be found in present existence but also the way in which sin and death can erode, if not destroy, the God-given meaningfulness of human life. They can choke the longing for ultimate union, for God. Our age presents multiple meanings but is any of them sufficient? Can they really fill the God-shaped void?

MEANING IN THE OLD TESTAMENT

In the biblical world, there is a sense in which meaning is already a given, and a sense where meaning is also frustrated. The Old Testament has a number of different ways, in different contexts, to speak of the quest for meaning and the longing for God. It is both a theological and moral quest. In the first Creation account, on the sixth day, the meaning is located in the "image of God" [whereby humankind's role is to fill the earth and take responsibility for it] including the creatures of the earth (Gen 1:26–28). The meaning thus bestowed in creation is severely damaged by human disobedience that creates enmity, pain, and struggle where there was none originally. From that point on, meaning becomes a difficulty, no longer effortless, no longer a simple gift.

God's redemptive power, however, creates new meaning with the establishing of God's people, Israel, and the gift and responsibilities of the covenant: through Abraham and Sarah, through Moses and the giving of the law, through the faithfulness of Ruth, through the covenant with David. Much of the Old Testament presents the history of Israel as the failure of that God-given meaning and the struggle to reclaim it in the prophetic voice, for example, calling out against idolatry and injustice. Amos expresses the meaning of Israel's life: "He has told you, O mortal, what is good; / and what does the LORD require of you but to do justice, and to love kindness, and to walk humbly with your God?" (Mic 6:8). Meaning for the people of God is to be rediscovered in justice, mercy and a humble relationship with God.

The desire for intimate connection to God, as well as to others and to creation, is intrinsic to this Old Testament vision. It comes about through the covenant and goes back to the psalms:

As a deer longs for flowing streams,
    so my soul longs for you, O God.
My soul thirsts for God,
    for the living God.
When shall I come and behold
    the face of God?

(Ps 42:1–2)

O God, you are my God, I seek you,
    my soul thirsts for you;
my flesh faints for you,
    as in a dry and weary land where there is no water.

(Ps 63:1)

This desire is the longing for God's salvation but also for God's nearness, for an awareness of a God who sometimes seems absent and for whose presence the psalmist deeply longs. Meaning is to be found in this quest and its fulfillment.

There is another sense in which meaning is also a future event, a restoration, the promise of God's future reign with the ending of all that frustrates meaning. Israel is to be reconstituted as the people of God (Ezek 37:7–14), the Law is to be written on their hearts, implying that no effort is needed for them to fulfill it (Jer 31:31–34), and harmony will be restored to Israel and to the whole earth (Isa 2:2–4; 11:6–9; 60:17—61:4; Mic 4:1–8). In these visions, creation is restored to what God intended, and its meaning reinstated.

The New Testament shares this future orientation, but sees it as being fulfilled with the coming of Jesus. Both Testaments share a primarily social focus, implying that meaning is found in, and related to, community. The New Testament writers, however, also emphasize the personal aspects of faith and meaning, and the longing for God. Although terminology for meaning is absent from these texts, the concept itself is implied in the understanding of salvation and the restoration of creation, and in the focus on relationship and divine presence. The frustration of meaning is resolved in the life, death, and resurrection of Jesus, who makes meaningful those lives that have been emptied by suffering, bereavement, sin, disability, and death. He himself embodies both the deepest longings for God and their fulfillment.

READING JOHN ARIGHT

The Gospel chosen for this exploration of the quest for meaning is the Gospel of John. Meaning is implied in John's understanding of the salvation that comes through Jesus' incarnation, ministry, death, and resurrection, where the longing for life and for God is fulfilled. John's particular focus on discipleship addresses, by implication, many of our contemporary concerns about meaning and its relationship to key Johannine concepts such as truth, love, peace, and joy.

In order to read John aright, however, as we have already noted,[8] we need to respect the degree of separation between his Gospel and that of the Synoptics. Even with the common elements between them, John is different from the other Gospels. It is indeed part of the strength of the Gospel canon that we are offered more than one perspective on Jesus and on discipleship. It is important, therefore, that we read John as an evangelist—a storyteller and theologian—in his own right. Attempts to harmonize John with the other Gospels are not helpful, since they detract from the uniqueness of John and dilute Johannine theology in favor of a bland conformity. If John is writing to complement— and perhaps even correct—the other Gospels, or gospel traditions, we need to allow him the space to do so, without imposing an artificial harmony on him or the other evangelists. Otherwise, we lose the diversity in a premature concern for the unity. There is a unity to be found but it is not something to be imposed or artificially constructed. In the end, all the Gospels attest to the one Christ and the one source of salvation and life, through his ministry, his suffering and death, and his resurrection.[9]

The Fourth Gospel, itself, gives us somewhat ambiguous information on the author, or the date and place of its composition. The character of "the disciple whom Jesus loved" creates more problems than it solves and, in effect, does nothing to resolve the anonymity of the Gospel. Tradition points to John the Apostle, the son of Zebedee and brother of James the Great,[10] though this is less likely, given the lateness of dating and the very different perspective the Fourth Gospel possesses from the other Gospels. Other possibilities for authorship are John the Elder, an eyewitness but not one of the Twelve,[11] or even an unknown disciple of a later generation.[12] Mostly, John is dated to the last decade of the first century, when Domitian was the Roman Emperor (AD 81–96), and Ephesus is the traditional location, a center of the cult of emperor worship. In the end, all we have is the Gospel itself and a measure of, one hopes, intelligent guesswork about its provenance, context, and authorship.

The issue we are addressing in this chapter opens a series of questions that we might bring to our reading of the Johannine text. Our concern is the questions we might ask the Gospel of John about our contemporary search for meaning, even though the terminology itself is lacking in the text. At the risk of stating the obvious, John is offering a religious and spiritual "answer" to our questions. He is not primarily concerned with other aspects of our lives that bestow undoubted meaning, though these lie within his wider comprehension. His concerns have more to do with questions of ultimacy and longing. Where might we locate a sense of ultimate meaning in the uniquely Johannine worldview? What symbols, narratives, and characters from this ancient text might convey a sense of meaning for us today? How can John assist us to rediscover meaning in our experience where it has been eaten away by sickness, disability, hunger, sin, grief, or death—in order to reignite the holy longing?

Two of the nearest conceptions to meaning in the Fourth Gospel are that of life and discipleship. These are expressions of John's spirituality. Though they are not synonymous with the idea of meaning, they consist of notions that are, from the Johannine point of view, inherently meaningful for human life. John unfolds both concepts through the narrative, which itself consists of images, symbols, and characterization, set against the background of Old Testament figures, feasts, and festivals.

JOHN AND LIFE

The language John uses throughout the Gospel to designate life is generally that of "eternal life" (*zôê aiônios*), a concept that needs careful understanding. In John's Gospel, everything is about the disclosure of life, eternal life. This life fills and makes meaningful the present moment, yet lasts for eternity. It is both a present possession and a future hope, and it overcomes death and all that is meant by "death," whether spiritual, moral, social, psychological, or physical. True life, for John, donates a rich and abundant sense of meaning to human life.

Eternal life in the Gospel of John is not simply a spiritual concept. It is also profoundly linked to creation and the life of the natural world. Life, all life, has its origins in God in the divine Word through whom all things were created. All that is good in creation comes from God: "All things came into being through him, and without him not one thing came into being. What has come into being in him was life" (1:3–4). John's Gospel begins, therefore, with God's good creation and the life which is given to all created things in and through the dynamic Word of God.[13]

Spirituality is inseparable from the inherently meaningful life of creation.

As with the first account of Creation in Genesis, the very first manifestation of life is light on the first day (Gen 1:4), even before the creation of the sun, moon, and stars on the fourth day (Gen 1:14–19): "and the life was the light of all people" (John 1:4). Clearly, we are not speaking here of the light of the sun, but the illumination given by God in every sense to humankind. That the image has metaphorical intent is made clear in the next verse where we find the darkness and the light in conflict, and the darkness unable to "grasp" it — unable either to comprehend or overpower it (1:5; the verb *overcome* contains both meanings). Almost from the start of the Gospel, John assumes without explanation the presence of malignant forces that would snuff out that primeval, created light.

John also quickly makes clear that the light is associated intimately with the Word who is the source of creation, who enters the world to illuminate those places that have fallen to the darkness (1:9–13), and who becomes incarnate in Jesus Christ (1:14–18). Later in the Gospel, Jesus will be revealed as the Light of the World, illuminating the lives of those who follow him so that they need no longer walk in the darkness (8:12; 9:5).

Entry into eternal life requires a new birth, just as ordinary human life (which equally has its origins in God) also requires birth. Jesus' encounter with Nicodemus explores the meaning of this new birth "from above," in which the Holy Spirit gives life to believers (3:3–10).[14] They become thereby the "children of God," recovering their lost identity in creation (1:12–13). Nicodemus, though a teacher in Israel (3:9), fails to understand the metaphor. In the discourse that follows, Jesus speaks of his coming as the result of the divine love and desire to bestow saving and illuminating life on all people, though some will tragically reject it and so condemn themselves to death and darkness (3:14–21).

John makes clear that the main purpose of Jesus' coming is precisely to give life, and therefore meaning, generously and profusely. Speaking as the Good Shepherd, Jesus offers the sheep—the people of God—authentic and copious life. This life nurtures the flock by day, offering plentiful pasture, and protects it by night within the safety of the fold: "I came that they may have life, and have it abundantly" (10:10). The protection of the sheep is a vital aspect of the life they receive, because of the deathly forces ranged against them: strangers, thieves, and bandits whose intent is only to kill and destroy. Elsewhere in the Gospel, John expresses this "life" in a variety of concepts: it brings peace and joy (4:27; 15:11), gives access to truth and love (8:31; 14:6; 15:9–10), and bestows a sense of homecoming and belonging (17:22–24; 19:26–27).

The last two miracles, the most spectacular in the Gospel, hone in on the imagery of light and life from the Prologue of the Gospel. In the healing of the man born blind, which is part of the Feast of Tabernacles,[15] Jesus creates the man's sight, a sight he has never possessed (9:1–7).[16] By the end of the narrative, when the man sees Jesus literally for the first time, after being rejected by the religious authorities, he also comes to see him metaphorically and spiritually; he recognizes Jesus as the Son of Man, the giver of life, a recognition that ends in worship (9:35–38). His life is illuminated both literally and spiritually; he receives the gift of sight and of insight, becoming a disciple of Jesus. His life, in other words, becomes suffused with meaning in ways that are physical, social, as well as spiritual.

The raising of Lazarus gives a new and more complex understanding of eternal life in the Gospel of John. This miracle story, the seventh in the series, brings the first half of the gospel narrative to its climax. Here Jesus reveals himself spectacularly as "the resurrection and the life," drawing Martha into a fuller understanding of Johannine faith and the meaning of the life that Jesus both brings and embodies (11:25–27). The same narrative, extending to Mary's anointing of Jesus' feet and the threat to Lazarus's life from the authorities (12:1–11), also sets in motion the passion narrative. Jesus quite literally brings Lazarus from death to life at the cost of his own life. The huge response of faith from the Jewish mourners leads the authorities to decide that Jesus is too great a threat to their authority and status and must go (11:45–53). Jesus himself will take the sorrowful journey to death but will also rise from the dead: "I lay down my life," he says, speaking as the Good Shepherd, "in order to take it up again" (10:17).

John's point in this climactic story is to demonstrate that the eternal life that Jesus confers on those who desire it and recognize their need of it overcomes all obstacles, even death itself. Meaning is not a temporary gift but an eternal one, beyond all forces of destruction. As "the resurrection and the life," Jesus gives a life beyond—though contiguous with—that of nature; this life now transcends death. It is life in the midst of death and life on the other side of death: life in spite of death. It is this life that Martha affirms in her confession of faith and that Mary also confirms in her anointing of Jesus' feet: bringing the odor of life into the dank place of death (12:1–8).[17]

In Jewish thinking, eternal life is bestowed in the realms beyond death, at the last judgment when God rewards the righteous and punishes the wicked (e.g., 2 Esd 2:20–24). In Pharisaic thought, this life means the resurrection of the righteous dead (see, for example, the debates in Mark 12:13–34). Martha exemplifies this kind of conventional belief, when Jesus assures her of her brother's rising from the dead. "I know that he will rise again in the resurrection on the last day," is her reply (11:24). Martha does not yet understand that resurrection is embodied and embedded in Jesus himself, and that Jesus already *is* the resurrection—not just for the future but for now.[18]

This perspective makes John's Gospel unique among the evangelists and other New Testament theologians: the conviction that resurrection is a present reality for believers and not just for the future. Eternal life, in other words, is as much a quality of life as a quantity and it begins in the here-and-now. It is not simply something reserved for the last day (5:24–25). The forces of death can already be overcome in daily living through the forces of resurrection life that are vibrantly present. Meaning is a gift granted in the present moment and assured, equally, for the future in and beyond death.

THE PASSION AND LIFE

The passion narrative, which is unmistakably a story about a death, and a horrifying death at that, is also and more fundamentally a narrative of life. Each of the symbols surrounding the crucifixion point to the theme of life coming through death, and uniquely through Jesus' death, including in relation to Jesus' enemies. The title on the cross, indicating the charge for which he is suffering, emphasizes the universal kingship of Jesus, an unintended example of an irony that has been present in the passion account from the beginning (19:19–23). The seamless robe for which the Roman soldiers cast lots signifies that cosmic unity and union—between Jesus and his God, and between Jesus and his disciples—that death cannot in any sense unpick (19:23–24).

Jesus' own way of dying confirms the overriding theme of life. The glory language associated with Jesus' death in earlier chapters (e.g., 3:14–15; 13:31–32; 17:1) has made it clear that this event of humiliation is, in God's hands, a moment of glory and glorification, for both God and Jesus. God is glorified in the revelation of God's true nature, and Jesus is glorified in his ascension to the Father, which is the true, inner meaning of the cross and closely linked to the divine love that is manifested in the glory. Readers enter the passion story with the language of love and glory ringing in their ears, knowing full well that the story that appears on the surface and that is real enough at one level and in its own terms—a story of humiliation and hatred—is contradicted by another, deeper narrative that will finally win out and become the true, divine chronicle of this event. The reader reads on two levels: the real versus the ironic, the human versus the divine, the humiliation and death versus the exaltation and life.

The same point is reinforced by the ambiguity of the wording of Jesus' actual death. His last cry is not one of abandonment, as in Mark and Matthew, but rather one of triumphant completion: "It is finished" (19:30). This is more than a statement of closure and ending—indeed, it is in no sense an ending at all—but rather articulates Jesus' knowledge of having achieved that for which he has come and the attainment of the divine will, in which he too shares. It signifies victory over evil and death, the overcoming of "the world."[19] John tells us that, bowing his head, Jesus then "gave up his spirit." The wording makes clear that Jesus, having uniquely divine power over life and death, surrenders his own life voluntarily (10:18). But it also suggests the giving of the Holy Spirit, the gift of life given in and through Jesus' death: "he handed over the Spirit" is equally possible as a translation (see 20:22).[20]

A similar focus is apparent in the interactions with the small band of disciples gathered at the foot of the cross. Once again, we confront symbols of vibrancy and life emerging from the very jaws of death. Jesus' gifting of his mother and his beloved disciple to one another is one such symbol (19:26–27). The precise meaning of this dialogue is often debated, but at the deeper level, it is clearly more than Jesus' personal concern for an aged mother and a bereft friend. Jesus has, after all, brothers to care for their mother, and the beloved disciple is not alone among the disciples. Even at the foot of the cross, in Peter's absence, he is accompanied by the women disciples, including Mary Magdalene. It is much more likely that Jesus indicates, here and now, the birth of the believing community, born out of his death, and formed by the loving and intimate union of these two key disciples, beyond the natural ties of family.[21]

The final image in the passion narrative is the flow of blood and water from the side of the crucified Jesus that, like most of the symbols, is uniquely Johannine (19:31–37). Here, the beloved disciple acts as the witness to Jesus' death and its saving, life-giving significance. While the soldiers are merely attempting to ensure Jesus' death and the authorities are interested only in their piety over the Passover feast, John's meaning is a deeper one. The witness language and two Old Testament quotations make it apparent that, for the evangelist, this death is redolent with life, life from death. Blood and water are both symbols of life through the Gospel, and here is no exception. In the association they have with birth, the two symbols reveal Jesus' death as life-giving, indeed as the source of life and salvation.[22] It is for this reason that the risen Christ will appear with his wounds intact (20:20, 25–27); his death is the source, and the only source, of life for his disciples. Through the meaningless event of the crucifixion, through Jesus' embrace of our darkness and meaninglessness, meaning is assured for disciples.

In summary, eternal life in John's Gospel is a gift in the here-and-now, just as creation is likewise a gift from the same divine source. Containing the seeds of resurrection, both now and at the end, eternal life overcomes evil, suffering, and death through the life-giving death of Jesus. This life is abundant, bountiful, rich, and fulfilling, giving safety and nurture. It enlightens the darkness of ignorance and sin, and sets free from all that binds and constricts (8:32–36), opening blind eyes to goodness and truth. It reveals a dimension beyond the present, one that ultimately transcends the limitations and mortality of creation, offering life in and beyond death. The Johannine Jesus, incarnate, crucified, and risen, is the source of that life, the Word who is the source of creation and who reveals himself, in his flesh, as resurrection and life. He gives eternal life, not simply as a free gift without cost, but by making his own journey from life to death and death to life in his passion. He is the seed that falls into the ground and dies, blossoming from the earth to produce abundant fruit and new life (12:24).

Eternal life and the meaning that emerges from it are attained, both in the present and for the future, in relationship with God through Jesus. It is the relationship itself that bestows this meaningful life, an internal rather than external affiliation: "And this is eternal life," says Jesus in his great prayer at the end of the Farewell Discourse and immediately before his arrest, "that they may know you, the only true God, and Jesus Christ whom you have sent" (17:3). Eternal life is the consequence of knowing God, knowing God in intimacy and love, and knowing therefore the Christ of God's sending as the self-revelation of that life-giving God.

DISCIPLESHIP AND FAITH

Eternal life as a present gift and future hope is discovered, in particular, through connection to Jesus, a connection attained through John's understanding of discipleship in the Fourth Gospel. There are several Johannine images that unfold this understanding of discipleship. The first of these is faith or, since John prefers the verb, *believing*.[23] To believe is the authentic response to Jesus' offer of eternal life, and it encapsulates the purpose of the Gospel (20:30–31). In most cases, it refers to believing in Jesus, which also means believing in God: "Whoever believes in me believes not in me but in him who sent me" (12:44). Believing is presented in the Gospel as a spectrum, since many of the characters of the Gospel are capable of growing in faith or retreating from it, as Jesus' self-revelation unfolds.

To believe means to open the heart in faith to the dual nature of revelation and the meaning it provides—the self-revealing of God in Jesus and the revealing of the self in dialogue with Jesus (4:16–26). The story of the Samaritan woman is the most obvious example of this dual focus of believing. The woman's faith grows as the revelation unfolds. It is the revelation of her own self: "Come and see a man who told me everything I have ever done!" she says to the townsfolk (4:29). It is also the revelation of Jesus' identity: "I am he, the one who is speaking to you," he says to her at the end of their conversation (4:26).

In John's Gospel, believing can be ambiguous. The most hostile section of the Gospel outside the passion narrative is the Tabernacles Discourse, a dialogue between Jesus and "the Jews" (7:1—8:59). Those who have come to believe reject Jesus and end up abusing him (8:59). In the previous narrative, many of those who believed in Jesus are so scandalized by his words that they lose faith and cease following him (6:66), until he is left only with the Twelve. Jesus does not always respond well to those who claim to believe. Faith based only on "signs" is inadequate, unless it can see beyond the "signs" to the divine glory they unveil in Christ. Believing is easily quenched and results in a tragic loss of meaning: "We have no king but the emperor" declare Jesus' opponents before Pilate, in a radical denial of their identity (19:15). Believing, as with unbelieving, determines one's identity in this Gospel and thus one's sense of meaning (3:14–18).

At the same time, believing is often partial and needs to grow. Martha, for example, makes the Christian confession, "I believe that you are the [Christ] Messiah" (11:27), but her faith wavers at the mouth of the tomb. Similarly, all the disciples need to move to Easter faith after the resurrection. The Johannine Jesus acts differently toward those who struggle with faith, as opposed to those who reject it outright. Believing needs to grow through experience. In those who truly desire to believe, the Johannine Jesus is patient and understanding, leading the believer to deeper levels of believing. Meaning is not a single, simple gift but rather something larger and deeper into which believers grow: the hope that life will finally win out over death, the conviction that God has infused all life with meaning.

DISCIPLESHIP AND ABIDING

The image of abiding is a second important term for discipleship in John's Gospel and is likewise concerned with the making and finding of meaning.[24] At the beginning of the Gospel, the two disciples of John the Baptist approach Jesus on the basis of the Baptist's testimony to the "Lamb of God" (1:29, 35), and ask the question: "Rabbi...where are you staying [*abiding*]?" (1:38). Jesus' reply, "Come and see" (1:39), is more than an invitation to inspect his home. The invitation, like the initial question, is filled with significance. To "abide" with Jesus is metaphorical for discipleship. The one on whom the Spirit abides ("remains," in most translations) draws disciples to abide with him and to discover life and meaning within that abiding relationship (1:33).

Similarly, the Samaritan villagers approach Jesus after the Samaritan woman's testimony (4:29, 39) and Jesus remains (*abides*) with them for two days (4:40). In Johannine terms, the verb suggests something more significant and symbolic. Jesus makes more than a two-day stay with the Samaritans. They have come to know him in a way that indicates their conversion to faith, their acceptance of Jesus as the Savior of the world, and their discovery of radically new levels of meaning to their faith. Like the woman herself, they too have become Jesus' disciples.

In John, the language of abiding is about discipleship and relationship, symbolized above all in the Eucharist (6:51–59). Sharing in the Eucharist through faith creates a mutual and deeply meaningful bond of *abiding* between Jesus and his disciples: "Those who eat my flesh and drink my blood abide in me, and I in them" (6:56). This bond parallels the abiding that exists between the Father and Jesus (6:57), where Jesus draws his disciples into his relationship with the Father.

At the heart of the Farewell Discourse in John is the symbol of the vine and the branches (15:1–17). The Johannine Jesus stands at the center of the abiding imagery, which is a life-giving and life-affirming symbol of life, joy, and meaning. Jesus is the Vine through which sap flows to the branches, enabling disciples to flourish in their lives and produce grapes for the harvest. The abiding of disciples on Jesus is based on the Son's abiding in the Father, and the Father's abiding in the Son—an abiding and a sense of ultimate meaning in which the Spirit also shares (1:32–33; 15:10).

The Johannine picture of abiding may seem at first a somewhat passive image of discipleship, but the evangelist describes it as fruitful and dynamic. In John, discipleship is not just about effort and struggle. The priority lies in relationship and mutual love within the community of faith, calling disciples into a given intimacy of family relationships. The making of meaning in the image of abiding is gift as well as search. Abiding focuses on the central role of the Johannine Jesus, who holds together the two threads, just as he holds the vine, giving life and meaning to those who rest in his love and presence.

DISCIPLESHIP AND LOVE

Abiding is closely linked to the idea of love, another Johannine image for discipleship and equally foundational to meaning. Images of love and friendship are common in the Fourth Gospel. The verb "to love" first appears in the dialogue with Nicodemus: "God so loved the world [literally, "loved the world in this way"] that he gave his only Son" (3:16). Jesus is referring to his own death, his "lifting up" on the cross (3:14–15), like the Exodus story in the wilderness where the rebellious Israelites, bitten by poisonous snakes sent by God in punishment, are saved by gazing on the bronze image of a serpent (Num 21:4–9). In both cases, the exaltation paradoxically (though for very different reasons!) brings healing and life. The crucifixion is the great sign of divine love through the incarnation. What the incarnation is about in the ministry of Jesus, the cross, and resurrection is the saving love of God that restores meaning to every human life.[25]

The love relationship between Father and Son, through the Spirit, is the basis of discipleship in this Gospel. In entering into

81

this preexistent love at the heart of creation, disciples regain their damaged or lost identity, and thus find true and authentic meaning, as the "children of God" (1:12). In entering the mutuality of divine love, they become not only children but also friends of God (15:15). In Johannine terms, friendship is another way of speaking about love. The members of the family from Bethany, for example, are friends of Jesus, those loved by him (11:3, 5). This is the language of discipleship. Jesus proves his friendship for Lazarus by raising him from the dead, and placing his own life in danger that will lead to the cross. Martha and Mary are "friends" of Jesus, disciples whose faith is challenged in this narrative. Mary expresses the authentic response of friendship and love in her anointing of Jesus' feet (12:1–8). She responds to the costliness of Jesus' gift of life with the gift of the perfumed oil, a perfume that pervades the house, overcoming the stench of death. Friendship with Jesus is life-giving for disciples, calling them into a meaningful relationship of mutual love and intimacy.

The image of abiding is closely tied to that of love and friendship. Abiding is really about friendship, a friendship that begins with Jesus himself and his love for his disciples, manifest above all in his loving and saving death: "Having loved his own who were in the world, he loved them to the end" (13:1). No longer are the disciples servants or slaves but loved and loving friends: "I do not call you servants [slaves] any longer, because the servant does not know what the master is doing; but I have called you friends, because I have made known to you everything that I have heard from my Father" (15:15).

The friends of Jesus are called not only into friendship with Jesus and thus with God, but also with one another, based in the love-command: "I give you a new commandment, that you love one another. Just as I have loved you, you also should love one another" (13:34). In this sense, meaning in the Fourth Gospel is profoundly linked to community on both vertical and horizontal planes. What is "new" about this command is the clause, "as I have loved you." The command is new because Jesus has bestowed the same love on his disciples who are held in it by his love and the love of the Father.[26] That is the essential command of this Gospel. Those who are embraced by the Father's love for the Son belong in a mutual relationship of love with God and one another.

The foot-washing demonstrates this understanding of the way in which meaning is to be found in love and friendship. For John, the foot-washing is symbolic of the cross that brings both cleansing and union with Jesus through his self-giving death. The cross, for John, is an act of glorification, the self-revelation of the Father's true nature in love for the world. Yet it is also an act of service on Jesus' part, service to "his own," those the Father has given him. The foot-washing is a symbolic act, pointing to the death of Jesus, by which the disciples are "cleansed" in order to enter into union with Jesus, and also a symbol of the self-giving love among the community of disciples (13:12–15). In this latter interpretation, foot-washing is a symbol of the love-command and is emblematic of the love that is to thrive among the community of friends, who are to love and serve one another, and to find meaning in doing so.

The gift of the mother of Jesus and the beloved disciple to each other at the foot of the cross is another symbolic action demonstrating the love and friendship of disciples (19:25–27). The relationship between these two figures in John's Gospel, neither of whom is named, is symbolic for the whole community of disciples. The mother of Jesus has already shown faith and trust in the word of Jesus (2:5), pointing to where ultimate meaning is located for the Johannine community. The beloved disciple is the true "friend of Jesus" in this Gospel, a title also given to John the Baptist (3:29–30).[27]

Jesus' dialogue with Simon Peter after his resurrection is also important in understanding love and friendship in this Gospel (21:15–19).[28] Jesus asks Peter three times to confirm his love, a love that exceeds everything else. Thus Jesus rehabilitates Peter after his threefold denial, reestablishing the love that once wavered but will now stand firm. Both his following of Jesus and shepherding of the Good Shepherd's flock are based on Peter's love for Jesus. That is to be the heart of his vocation, the center of his being. For John, not only Peter but also disciples in general are called to the same love and friendship; they too are called to be "beloved disciples," to be the friends of Jesus and friends to one another even to the point of giving up their lives. The

Johannine understanding of love and friendship both gives and demands all. Ironically, finding meaning in John's Gospel can lead to martyrdom and death.

DISCIPLESHIP AND FOLLOWING

The imagery of following is not as common in the Gospel of John as in the Synoptic Gospels, though it is still present and still a vital image expressing both the gift and the struggle to make meaning. The Gospel begins and ends with images of following: the two disciples who "come and see" at the beginning (1:38–39) and Peter who is called to follow at the end of the Gospel (21:22). The story of Philip being called by Jesus to "follow" suggests that John knows the Synoptic tradition where the first disciples are called directly by Jesus. The image of following appears several times throughout the ministry of Jesus. At the Feast of Tabernacles, Jesus as the Light of the world calls people to discipleship, promising illumination to those who follow him (8:12). "Following" is an image of the love and trust the sheep have for the Good Shepherd (10:4, 16, 27). In response to the coming of the Greeks, Jesus declares that following him means service, and service as an intrinsic part of meaning implies losing life in order to "keep it for eternal life" (12:25).

The same idea of following appears in the passion narrative. Simon Peter attempts to follow Jesus after his arrest (18:15) but fails dismally and instead denies Jesus three times (18:15–18, 25–27). After the resurrection, Jesus completes his dialogue with Peter with the simple command, "Follow me" (21:19), a command that will take him to a martyr's death. Peter is now to follow faithfully the risen Christ. Following is based on personal attachment in love and trust, a love that is prepared to face death for Jesus' sake and the sake of the flock. At the heart of following is love, the motivating force in the relation between Jesus and his disciples. Following Jesus means a close, intimate attachment to him. Just as Mary of Bethany gives a costly gift to Jesus in the anointing (12:1–8), so Johannine disciples are called to give themselves to him entirely. Like Mary Magdalene in the Easter garden, they learn to recognize the voice of the Good Shepherd calling their names, filling them with love and meaning, and sending them out to proclaim his risen life (20:16–18).[29]

Discipleship in the Fourth Gospel arises from the prior relationship of the Son to the Father. The Son is sent to do the Father's will, abides in the Father, and his love for the Father is the basis of his identity and mission. The Spirit, too, belongs in the same circle of love and friendship that is the ultimate goal of meaning, as of life itself. Jesus calls disciples to enter that divine circle of meaning, opening the way to the Father's love and life. John's understanding of discipleship has its roots in contemplation: in worship, restful abiding, meditative love, and the embrace of God in the life of the believing community. As beloved disciples and friends of Jesus, future believers are called to receive that benediction (20:29), sharing in the same love as the original disciples to enter that divine life and meaning that lie at the heart of the universe.

LONGING IN JOHN

As well as meaning, the theme of longing is also present in John's narrative and connected to its understanding of eternal life and discipleship. It is most apparent in the story of the Samaritan woman's discovery of faith and life, which we have already touched upon. The imagery revolves around the well, which provides water for the village, its people and animals, and quenches their physical thirst. To this place Jesus travels from Judea (taking the unusual and more direct route through Samaria that his fellow countryfolk generally avoided), arriving in the middle of the day, hot, weary, and thirsty, and meets the woman (4:4–6).

At first, Jesus is the thirsty one and the woman is the water-giver; she has the bucket and therefore access to the deep well. But that scenario is soon overturned. Jesus reveals himself to be the giver of life-giving water that quenches, in a radical way, the thirst for life (4:13–14). It takes the woman some time to recognize both her own thirst and Jesus' identity as the water-giver, and when she does so, she brings with her the townsfolk. Though outsiders, they come to recognize in Jesus the "Savior of the world" (4:42). Through the universal need for water, Jesus is acclaimed the universal Savior, the one who fulfills (for everyone everywhere, regardless of race, culture, or gender) the deepest yearnings for life.[30]

The quenching of such a thirst is associated, for John, not just with Jesus but also with the Spirit. At the Feast of Tabernacles—where water (along with light) is a major symbol—Jesus summons those who are thirsty to drink of the water he provides (7:37–38). In words that recall both the gift of an internal spring of water (4:14) and the flow of blood and water from Jesus' crucified side (19:34), John adds: "Now he said this about the Spirit, which believers in him were to receive; for as yet there was no Spirit, because Jesus was not yet glorified" (7:39). While the sense of longing reaches for a world beyond the present age, it can nonetheless be accessed already through the presence and gift of the Spirit-Paraclete (14:16–17).[31]

For John, to seek Jesus authentically is to seek the fulfillment of the longing for true life. It is already present , as we have seen, in the coming of the first two disciples, when Jesus asks them the loaded question: "What are you looking for?" (1:38). Later, the crowds are seeking Jesus following the Feeding, but Jesus challenges them to seek not for "the food that perishes, but for the food that endures for eternal life" (6:27), which Jesus alone can give because he is "the bread of life" (6:35). Marking the end of his public ministry, Greeks approach Philip with the request, "Sir, we wish to see Jesus" (12:21). The coming of the Gentiles, seeking life, fulfillment, and salvation in Christ is the signal Jesus needs for the coming of the "hour," the time of his departure; his mission has been fulfilled (12:23).[32]

Behind the human quest for the God revealed in Jesus throughout John's Gospel lie Jesus' own hunger and thirst. This is more than a biological need in the narrative contexts in which it appears. Jesus' physical thirst, as we have seen, is transformed to become a vehicle for revealing the woman's thirst and his own capacity to quench it. Later, when the disciples return to the well with the food they have purchased, Jesus bewilders them by responding, "I have food to eat that you do not know about"

(4:32), adding by way of clarification, "My food is to do the will of him who sent me and to complete his work" (4:34). On the cross he experiences a raging thirst: "I am thirsty" (19:28), which is but one word in Greek (*dipso*). Once again, we recognize in Jesus a genuine physical need that nonetheless points to a spiritual passion for the will of God, a yearning to carry out God's will and to bestow meaning, a yearning that enables him to take the cup and not bypass it (18:11). It is the same zeal by which he cleanses the temple, the house of his Father (2:17).

Behind this longing, in turn, lies the desire of the Father who, in and through the ministry of Jesus, seeks out the human heart. This disclosure is made by Jesus at the well in a characteristically Johannine statement of God's future that is radically anticipated in the present: "But the hour is coming, and is now here, when the true worshipers will worship the Father in spirit and truth, for the Father seeks such as these to worship him" (4:23). The human longing mirrors the divine longing that has the priority, both in time and significance. Indeed, for John, salvation lies in the way that the yearning for meaning and for connection with God arises from God's own yearning for union with the creation: "that they may be one, as we are one" (17:22).

INTERROGATING JOHN

The questions proposed earlier for the Johannine evangelist centered around where in the Gospel, in its various literary devices (symbolism, narrative, characterization), we might find a sense of ultimate meaning that would have the capacity to speak to us today, particularly—though not only—in contexts of distressing experience, whether caused by misfortune, other people, or ourselves. We do so with the awareness that the language of meaning is our own and not John's, but with the conviction that, despite that, John's Gospel may still be able to speak to our own concerns across the centuries.

Though written from a devoutly Jewish perspective, Viktor Frankl's reflections on the pursuit of meaning, forged in the crucible of intense suffering and deprivation, find a strange echo

in the Gospel of John. At one point, while working in the darkness of early morning digging a trench in the icy cold, Frankl has
a kind of epiphany: "At that moment a light was lit in a distant
farmhouse, which stood on the horizon as if painted there, in the
midst of the miserable grey of a dawning morning in Bavaria.
'*Et lux in tenebris lucet*' — and the light shineth in the darkness."[33]
Frankl sees that illumination and sense of meaning as existing
primarily in the experience and recollection of love — again a
theme he shares with the Gospel of John.

This experience reflects the possibility of a meaning to be
found in — or, in some cases, in spite of — the specific realities of
an otherwise meaningless context. The gift of life, eternal life, in
John's Gospel conveys a similar sense: "the Johannine idea of life
can only be understood and proclaimed where people are still
searching for the meaning of human life."[34] This is far from the
shadowy, nebulous promise of a life beyond this one, a life on
the other side of death. John describes eternal life as something
offered in the present moment, something that does indeed transcend death but that also invades and radiates present experience.
"In the world you face persecution," Jesus says to the disciples,
dismayed at the prospect of his departure, "but take courage; I
have conquered the world" (16:33).[35] Here, the gift Jesus gives is
that of peace, but it is an unusual kind of peace, a peace donated
in the midst of its apparent opposite, conflict and trouble: "Peace
I leave with you; my peace I give to you. I do not give to you as
the world gives. Do not let your hearts be troubled" (14:27). This
peace comes from a sense of meaning that cannot be destroyed by
anything a hostile, unbelieving world can concoct.

Meaning involves a sense of identity, of knowing who we
are, and where and to whom we belong. In human terms, that
question can be answered at one level in terms of family and
friends, work and vocation. And yet, ultimately, that answer
is not enough. Family and friends can be lost, through tragedy
or conflict; employment and health can be likewise lost; we can
indeed lose everything. If our identity is to hang only on those
aspects of our lives that can be taken from us, our foundations are
not strong enough to withstand the day of trouble or any serious
loss. Nor can these things fill the deeper emptiness from which
the longing for connection to a transcendent mystery arises.

The identity that John offers in his Gospel, without denying the worth and value of these other dimensions of our identity, is something that underlies all the rest. In the Johannine Jesus, we are offered the restoration of an ancient identity, partially lost or obscured by life-denying forces that have, knowingly or unknowingly, risen against us—obscuring the connection with a deeper and more sublime reality. That primeval identity is as children of God. And it is an identity that can never be lost, whatever else may happen to us. It is the basis of an abiding and perpetual meaning or, in John's terms, everlasting life. This meaning, this life, encircles all the other meanings, all the other ways we find life, injecting them with an eternal significance and sense of fulfillment. Because of this unfathomable meaning, we can grasp the divine peace in times of conflict and tribulation, we can know joy even in sorrow, we can hold to what is genuine in a world of counterfeits and fraud. This level of meaning is something that we can grasp and hold onto—or, better still, it is an identity that grasps hold of us and does not let us go, does not allow us to sink into a pit of meaninglessness and insignificance.

This identity forms the basis of our self-confidence, which itself infuses our lives with meaning. All the forms of self-hatred—low self-worth, harsh judgmentalism toward ourselves, the immobilizing dread of our own gifts and competencies—deprive our lives of meaning, making our lives seem worthless. Our reclaimed identity as children of God, and the task of growing more fully and completely into that identity, is the best foundation for self-esteem. It is not grounded in lies or image or cultural markers of external success, but on something that can survive even the crumbling of images, defeat, and failure. Here again, this kind of meaning, this identity, is given as a gift and not dependent on secondary influences or the fluxes in our transient lives.

As well as identity, the quest for meaning also involves "the motivational force" in our lives.[36] In other words, we need something that is ontologically given but that is also a motivating force; we need both being and task; identity and struggle:

> What man [sic] actually needs is not a tensionless state
> but rather the striving and struggling for a worthwhile

89

goal, a freely chosen task. What he needs is not the discharge of tension at any cost but the call of a potential meaning waiting to be fulfilled by him.[37]

This is where John's variegated understanding of discipleship comes in. John is well aware that discipleship involves striving and endeavor. He speaks of the branches on the vine being pruned, although the actual verb he uses is "cleansed" (15:2–3). This is not a theology of works replacing grace. The grace, itself, is a given, freely and generously bestowed in the repaired identity of the children of God. What grace calls forth is the struggle to become disciples, to grow more fully into that God-given identity. Again and again throughout the Fourth Gospel, we find characters struggling to understand—often going awry, but in many cases, finally attaining the truth for which they are striving. The Samaritan woman is one such example, as is the man born blind (4:16–26; 9:24–38). Mary Magdalene's struggle to find the "body" of her Lord is rewarded in the end with the sight of his risen presence and the commission to proclaim the resurrection; but it is attained through tears, mistaken turnings, and misapprehensions (20:11–18).

The call to believe and abide in, to love and follow Jesus, is inventive, providing the motivational force that is itself constitutive of meaning. To undertake this faith journey in growing dependence on God, in an expansive spirit of love, is to walk beside the one who is the way, the truth, and the life (14:6), the one whose leading illuminates the darkness and fills with meaning the life of disciples, fulfilling their deepest and most lasting desires. Once more, this is a motivation and a meaning that no force of circumstance can destroy, because it is grounded in the eternal things.

The sense of a holy longing is implied in the Gospel particularly in the language of seeking and finding.[38] That seeking is not confined to the earthly sphere but originates "from above": both Jesus and the Father are also on a quest to seek and find those who will believe, a quest that embraces the readers of the Gospel.[39] They can identify with Philip, who is "found" by Jesus (1:43–45); they belong among the sheep who find true pasture in him (10:9). There are admittedly also those who seek in the wrong place or with the wrong motivation, and for them, there is no assurance of finding (5:39, 44; 7:34; 8:21), no satisfaction for a longing they may not recognize. But for those who are open and genuinely questing, there is an assured finding, and a rich and abiding sense of belonging to be discovered, an emptiness that fills the void. The human longing for God, for authentic life and union, begins in God's own longing for union with the creation, reaching out to draw all creation into the one embrace—the one, divine plenitude.

It is true that this sense of holy longing—our seeking of the divine grounded in the divine seeking of us—is not only confined to Christianity but is present also in other religions' traditions.[40] Although the imagery differs, there is also a common element to them all:

> The seeker yearns to touch that which is just out of reach or to see that which is just out of sight. In this way, our holy longing points the way toward an image of god, and it, in turn, can guide us in the direction of the ineffable, ungraspable, unknowable realm behind the image.[41]

John's Gospel acknowledges the transcendence of a God who is unseen and unknown ("No one has ever seen God," 1:18), but it is also very clear about the shape and direction of the imagery, and sees these as ultimately irreducible. The "image" or face of God in this Gospel is Jesus Christ, the Word made flesh, who incarnates the divine longing for union and makes it possible for human beings to identify the longing and so cross the wide and deep abyss between Creator and creation. Jesus' life in the Gospel of John demonstrates this divine longing, and also the confrontation it involves with those who would quench it entirely or fill it with dross. Jesus' death illustrates that the fulfillment of the longing is costly: a burning up, a consuming in the fire of love and light, for Jesus himself and also for his followers (12:23–32; 21:15–19).

"THE SELFISH GIANT"

There is a children's tale written by Oscar Wilde (1854–1900) that captures something of the dynamic of John's emphasis on life, both in the here-and-now and in the world to come. "The Self-ish Giant" is one of a series of five stories written specifically for children that Wilde published in 1888 under the title *The Happy Prince and Other Tales,* when his two sons (Cyril and Vyvyan) were very young.[42] The volume represents something of a depar-ture from Wilde's previous writings (poetry and essays on art), yet it also coincides with the most productive and successful period of his literary career.

The main character in the story has been absent from his castle for some years and returns to find that children have been playing happily in his beautiful garden in the afternoons after school. The giant is horrified and chases them away, erecting a grim sign forbidding trespassing. Thereafter, spring comes to the world outside but not to the garden itself; it remains embed-ded in winter and the only occupants are the rain and hail, the snow and frost, and the harsh, cold winds.

One morning, the giant looks out his window to see that the children have crept back into the garden and are playing in the branches of the trees. Spring has come with them, along with the birds. What particularly catches his attention, however, is a small boy who is weeping because he cannot reach a tree that is still covered in snow. The sight melts the giant's hard heart. He runs outside and lifts the boy gently into the tree.

From that time on, the giant opens his garden to the chil-dren. He is transformed. He now loves to see them play in his garden and sits outside to watch them, enjoying with the children the beauty of his garden through all the seasons of the year. But he looks in vain for the small child he first met and misses him.

One day many years later, the giant looks out his window and sees the child beneath one of the trees. Strangely, the tree is in bloom with fruit on it, despite the fact that it is winter. The giant goes out joyfully to meet the boy and sees to his dismay that there are wounds on the boy's hands and feet. "These are the wounds of love," says the boy in answer to the giant's angry question.

"You let me play once in your garden," the child continues. "Today you shall come with me to my garden, which is Paradise."

When the children arrive later that day, they find the giant lying dead beneath the tree, covered in white blossom.

The novelist, Jeanette Winterson, believes that this and Wilde's other children's tales should receive wider recognition for their depth and literary qualities. She comments that "The Selfish Giant" is the most overtly Christian of all Wilde's children's tales, particularly with the Christ-figure of the little child.[43] The story is full of oppositions. The initial selfishness of the giant contrasts with his later generosity, the perpetual grip of winter is compared with the flowing movement of the seasons toward spring and summer, the wounds the giant inflicts on the children through his selfishness are reflected in the little boy's scarred hands and feet, white snow is replaced by white blossom, the giant's garden is a shadow of Christ's own garden, and love stands over against hate, beauty against ugliness, death against life.

Partly this is a moral tale: the giant finds life and meaning in generosity, in the opening of his garden to the laughter and play of happy children. But it is more than that. It is not the children in general who transform the giant but the Christ-child in particular. The recognition of the hands and feet, wounded by self-sacrificing love—signifying the incarnation—enable the giant's transition from death to life, from the garden of this world to the garden of the next, which are both places of beauty, fecundity, and happiness. This is a story about the discovery of true life and meaning, a meaning that transforms the present moment and that holds fast for the future on the other side of death—a transfigured life both within and beyond the present.

Winterson goes further in her interpretation of this tale, arguing that the high walls built around the garden, the hoarding and selfishness and the absence of spring find a parallel in Wilde's own dislike of industrial materialism: "Wilde hated the hoarding and excesses of his epoch's materialism—not because he was a socialist, but because his whole endeavour, his cult of art and beauty, was a fight against the coarsening of the soul."[44] The love of beauty for its own sake, apart from any kind of pragmatism or utility was, for Wilde, intrinsic to his sense of meaning in living.

Oddly enough, the parallels with Wilde's own subsequent biography continue in an inverted way and the image of the garden recurs. His own earlier career and the pursuit of beauty and pleasure gave way to an intense experience of suffering that he narrates in *De Profundis*, a letter written toward the end of his imprisonment in "The Ballad of Reading Gaol." He speaks of having "confined myself so exclusively to the trees of what seemed to me the sunlit side of the garden, and shunned the other side for its shadow and its gloom." However, he continues: "I don't regret for a single moment having lived for pleasure.... But...I had to pass on. The other half of the garden had its secrets for me also."[45] The experience of intense suffering, unjust imprisonment with the hard labor that broke his health, social disgrace, and financial ruin and destitution, led him finally to his own conversion and baptism as a Roman Catholic on his deathbed. In the depths of his suffering, Wilde paradoxically found a sense of life in the vision of Christ and the longing for a life within and beyond the natural world.

The story of the giant whose life and garden are transformed by the presence of the wounded Christ-child is a parable of the transformation of life in the midst of death and the longing for life. It understands that that transformation, ironically enough, occurs in and through death: the seed that is buried and rises from the earth, or the bronze serpent that heals those dying of snakebite. Like John's Gospel, it speaks of a life that can make all the difference to the present moment, filling it with meaning and also longing, even in the most adverse circumstances, even in the face of death itself. This, itself, can be a bittersweet experience. Even when the garden has been opened to the children, the giant looks to see the Christ-child again—the one who first opened his heart to the children yet who subsequently vanishes. There is a new and painful longing that accompanies his discovery of joy.

At the end, the giant's body, covered in white blossom from the garden he learned to share with others, and destined for another garden, is a symbol of a life that rises triumphant over meaninglessness, emptiness, and death, giving significance and meaning where otherwise none could exist. It is about a longing that is finally fulfilled, a garden of which his is only a shadow. Alongside John's Gospel, the story of the selfish giant makes a powerful point about the gift of life offered in the self-giving of the incarnate Christ and the fulfilling of the human longing for authentic life.

CONCLUSION

John's Gospel may not speak overtly of the quest for meaning or the longing for transcendence, but its theological and spiritual impetus implies these at every turn. In the language and concepts associated with eternal life, the Fourth Gospel offers human beings a profound sense of identity in recovering their true selves as beloved children of God, born of the Divine Spirit. The various images of discipleship—and particularly believing, abiding, loving, and following—offer the motivation that itself gives rise to a profound sense of meaning. Both dimensions, the quest for identity and the search for meaningful activity, are encompassed in the Fourth Gospel. The seeking for true life is fulfilled in Jesus—in other words, in the Father's seeking of true worshippers to share in the intimate relationship within the Trinity. What John offers is a meaning that cannot be thwarted or overthrown in times of trouble or tribulation, in sorrow or distress, in life or death. This meaning is an abiding one, a meaning that endures even in and beyond the grave, holding, sustaining, fulfilling, and nurturing eternal life in those who have become God's children. For them, seeking means finding and meaning is assured, given by and upheld in divine hands, in the present age as much as in the age to come.

Notes

1. Viktor E. Frankl, *Man's Search for Meaning* (Boston: Beacon Press, 1992), 98. The book was originally written (in German) immediately after the Second World War and published in 1946.
2. Ibid., 76.
3. "The Weight of Glory," a sermon originally preached by C. S. Lewis at St. Mary the Virgin, Oxford, June 8, 1942, 3, http://www.verber.com/mark/xian/weight-of-glory.pdf.
4. St. Augustine, *The Confessions*, trans. M. Boulding (New York: New City Press, 2014), Book I.1 (p. 39).

5. Kenneth Graham, *The Wind in the Willows* (London: Book Club Associates, 1977), 7.

6. Connie Zweig, *The Holy Longing: Spiritual Yearning and Its Shadow Side* (Bloomington: iUniverse, 2008), e-book loc. 396.

7. Ibid., loc. 385.

8. See introduction, pp. xx–xxi.

9. Richard A. Burridge speaks helpfully of the many portraits but the one Jesus (*Four Gospels, One Jesus?* [Grand Rapids, MI: Eerdmans, 2005], 164–82).

10. For example, Andreas J. Köstenberger, *John*, BECNT (Grand Rapids: Baker Academic, 2004), 6–8.

11. See Richard Bauckham, *The Testimony of the Beloved Disciple: Narrative, History, and Theology in the Gospel of John* (Grand Rapids, MI: Baker Academic, 2007), 73–91.

12. The question is linked to the anonymous presence and role of the mysterious Beloved Disciple; see, for example, Andrew T. Lincoln, *The Gospel According to Saint John*, BNTC (London: Continuum, 2005), 17–25. As Francis J. Moloney points out, we cannot finally be sure of the authorship, but that should make no difference to the significance of the Gospel (*The Gospel of John* [Collegeville, MN: Liturgical Press, 1998], 6–9).

13. On the creation theology inherent in the Gospel of John, see Mary E. Coloe, "Theological Reflections on Creation in the Gospel of John," *Pacifica* 24 (2011): 1–12.

14. "Born from above" is a better rendering of the Greek than "born again," though there is a sense of a second birth; the main emphasis is on the creative role of the Spirit (see Brendan Byrne, *Life Abounding: A Reading of John's Gospel* [Collegeville, MN: Liturgical Press, 2014], 65–66).

15. The central images of the tabernacles are water and light, both of which John uses metaphorically to speak of Christ as the fulfillment of this and other Jewish feasts.

16. Here Jesus is acting as the eternal Word, the source of creation, a view that goes back to Irenaeus (Mark Edwards, *John through the Centuries*, BBC [Oxford: Blackwell, 2004)], 99).

17. On the symbolic significance of Mary's anointing, see Dorothy A. Lee, *Flesh and Glory: Symbol, Gender and Theology in the Gospel of John* (New York: Crossroad, 2002), 197–211.

18. Given Martha's recoiling at the opening of the tomb (11:39), some argue that she has not as yet come to full faith; see Moloney, *Gospel of John*, 327–33, 339. Nevertheless, she like other disciples in John's Gospel grows in faith, and her belief in Jesus develops significantly in this narrative (see Lee, *Flesh and Glory*, 218–19, and F. Dale Bruner, *The Gospel of John: A Commentary* [Grand Rapids, MI: Eerdmans, 2012], 672–74, 680–81).

19. Judith Kovacs, "'Now shall the ruler of this world be driven out': Jesus' Death as Cosmic Battle in John 12:30–36," *Journal of Biblical Literature* 111 (1995): 227–47.

20. For this view, see Moloney, *Gospel of John*, 504–5, 508–9.

21. R. Alan Culpepper, *The Gospel and Letters of John* (Nashville: Abingdon, 1998), 232–34, and Jo-Ann A. Brant, *John* (Grand Rapids, MI: Baker Academic, 2011), 256–57. This view is reinforced if the mother of Jesus here also is a New Eve (Byrne, *Life Abounding*, 318–19). For a discussion of the possible meanings, see Lee, *Flesh and Glory*, 152–57.

22. On birth imagery here, see Lee, *Flesh and Glory*, 157–59.

23. Further on this theme, see Dorothy A. Lee, *Hallowed in Truth and Love: Spirituality in the Johannine Literature* (Melbourne/Eugene, OR: Mosaic/Wipf & Stock, 2011–12), 135–40.

24. See Lee, *Flesh and Glory*, 88–99.

25. Further on love as a central theme in John, see Francis J. Moloney, *Love in the Gospel of John: An Exegetical, Theological, and Literary Study* (Grand Rapids, MI: Baker Academic, 2013), esp. 99–133.

26. The Old Testament has its own love-command (Lev 19:18); see C. K. Barrett, *The Gospel According to St. John* (London: SPCK, 1978), 451–52.

27. On the parallels between John the Baptist and the Beloved Disciple in John's narrative, see Dorothy A. Lee, "Witness in the Fourth Gospel: John the Baptist and the Beloved Disciple as Counterparts," *Australian Biblical Review* 61 (2013): 1–17.

28. There is debate over whether John 21 was part of the original Gospel or was added later, either in a second edition or by a disciple of the author. Contrast the opposing views in Francis J. Moloney, "John 21 and the Johannine Story," in *Anatomies of Narrative Criticism: The Past, Present, and Futures of*

the Fourth Gospel as Literature, ed. Tom Thatcher and Stephen D. Moore (Atlanta: SBL, 2008), 237–51, and R. Alan Culpepper, "Designs for the Church in the Imagery of John 21:1–14," in *Imagery in the Gospel of John: Terms, Forms, Themes, and Theology of Johannine Figurative Language,* ed. Jörge Frey, Jan van der Watt, and Ruben Zimmermann, WUNT 200 (Tübingen: Mohr Siebeck, 2006), 369–72.

29. On following in John, see Lee, *Hallowed,* 155–58.

30. On the gender aspects of the story within its own cultural context, see Jerome H. Neyrey, "What's Wrong with This Picture? John 4, Cultural Stereotypes of Women, and Public and Private Space," in *A Feminist Companion to John,* ed. Amy-Jill Levine (London: Sheffield Academic Press, 2003), 1:98–125.

31. Further on the Spirit as "the Paraclete" in John, see, for example, Craig S. Keener, *The Gospel of John: A Commentary* (Peabody: Hendrickson, 2003), 2:953–82.

32. For example, Moloney, *Gospel of John,* 359; and Keener, *Gospel of John,* 2:871–72.

33. Frankl, *Man's Search for Meaning,* 40.

34. Rudolf Schnackenburg, *The Gospel According to St. John* (London: Burns & Oates, 1980), 2:361.

35. John's use of "the world" has to be carefully interpreted. It does not mean creation as such (which is the work of God) but, as often in the Farewell Discourse, the realm of death and darkness to which human beings are subject. Human beings themselves are embraced by God's love (3:16). See Keener, *Gospel of John,* 1:329–30.

36. Frankl, *Man's Search for Meaning,* 98.

37. Ibid., 104.

38. On the quest stories in John's Gospel, see John Painter, *The Quest for the Messiah: The History, Literature and Theology of the Johannine Community* (Edinburgh: T&T Clark, 1991), 1–25, 313–26.

39. Examples can be found at John 1:43; 4:23; 5:14, 30; 8:50; 9:35; 11:17; 12:14.

40. Zweig, *Holy Longing,* loc. 540–631.

41. Ibid., loc. 794.

42. Oscar Wilde, "The Selfish Giant," in *Collected Works of Oscar Wilde: The Complete Plays, Poems and Stories* (Ware, Hertsfordshire: Wordsworth Editions, 1997), 333–38.

43. "Why We Need Fairy Tales: Jeanette Winterson on Oscar Wilde," in *The Guardian*, October 17, 2013, http://www.theguardian.com/books/2013/oct/16/jeanette-winterson-fairytales-oscar-wilde.

44. Ibid.

45. *De Profundis*, in Wilde, *Collected Works*, 1080.

Chapter 4

DIVINE PURPOSE AND THE GOSPEL OF LUKE

CONTEXT

The core question being addressed to the Gospel of Luke is whether there is any sense of a divine purpose to human history, a purpose to which we have some access and in which we may participate. In some ways, this is a variation on the question of meaning that we directed to John's Gospel. This time, however, it has a wider canvas. It is not simply the quest for personal meaning but a broader, cosmic view. Does human history—and, for that matter, the history of creation—consist of a series of random events, culminating in the arbitrary position in which we now happen to exist, or is there a sense of a transcendent purpose wending its way in and through history and the processes of creation?

These are vast theological questions that touch on many aspects of faith. They are linked to the question of suffering, which we addressed to Mark's Gospel in the first chapter. If history is filled with violence and tragedy, how can it be said to contain a divine purpose? If people's lives seem more the result of chance than anything else, how can we identify these chance events with a divine purpose underlying them? If life is limited by social, cultural, and religious constraints—not to mention constraints of gender, family, or personality—how might these communicate a godly sense of purpose? If abuse, violence, and neglect are intrinsic to the story of creation, where do we locate the inherent creative finger of God?

In particular, these issues touch on the question of our participation in that purpose, if such purpose exists. Can we affect it, or is it beyond us in the sense that everything is already determined ("whatever will be, will be")? Does prayer make a difference? The issue here is not so much whether God exists but whether God is intimately involved in human history and the life of creation, and responsive to our (and its) needs. Has God wound up the world like an old-fashioned timepiece and set it ticking, leaving us (and it) to our own devices? Does God intervene in creation and in human affairs in response to our prayers? And, if so, why not intervene at once in answer to our prayers and put a definitive end to sin, evil, death, violence, and injustice?

There is a confrontative challenge in this last question that is addressed directly to God. It is as if we believe that the deity should intervene in human affairs and put an end immediately, without further ado, to all that is destructive in the world. And, if God does not automatically answer these prayers of ours, it must indicate either that God is not involved, not present, or that God is only present to some and not to others—to some contexts of injustice and not to others, to some privileged people who have prayed and not to others (some of whom may have prayed anyway). We end up either with a noninvolved God—a "noninterventionist" God—or an arbitrary God who plays favorites.

Yet the very question of whether or not God is an interventionist God is based on certain presuppositions, just as is the hostility against a God who will not intervene, except for the privileged few. It assumes that God stands entirely outside the universe, and from there, is capable—even if not always willing—to lend a sovereign helping hand from time to time. It may be that the language itself, and the questions themselves, need further refinement before we can ask them. To ask if God answers prayers in response to our needs assumes we know what "the answer" is or should be. But what if God is already present to the world, always present to it? What if God's ultimate purpose is not yet fully revealed and any answers we give may need to be provisional for that very reason?

Christian theology states that God has donated humankind with free will. John Polkinghorne, a distinguished scientist and theologian who has written extensively on the question of God and science, has expressed his conviction in this way:

> The creation of the God whose nature is love will not be a kind of cosmic puppet theatre in which the divine Puppet-Master pulls every string. The gift of love is always the gift of some due form of independence granted to the beloved....God is not a mere spectator of this process..., but neither are creatures caught up willy-nilly in a process in which they have no active part to play.[1]

This perspective is similar to that of David Bentley Hart, which we encountered in the first chapter on suffering and the Gospel of Mark. Hart speaks of "the mystery of created freedom" and "the union of free spiritual creatures with the God of love" as something that underlies the world's existence. Not only human beings but also, more widely, creation itself participates in this God-given freedom.[2]

As with our first chapter, however, we find ourselves in a somewhat agnostic position regarding these questions. We do not have definitive answers to all the questions of purpose and participation in the ongoing divine act of creation, especially to the question of "how" God is involved or "how" prayer actually works. Our answers, for that reason, are bound to be limited. But that does not mean we have no answers to give or that we are left, disconcertingly and disconsolately, with a large, white question mark hovering in the sky that slowly dissipates with the wind. We do have answers of a kind, but perhaps they are closer to metaphor than to bald, so-called scientific facts that can be proved or disproved.[3] We cannot prove that God is involved in our history and creation and invites our participation in its renewal, nor whether our prayers make a difference, but we can believe and act and go on praying anyway.

PURPOSE IN THE BIBLICAL WORLD

That there is a purpose to human history and creation is everywhere apparent in the biblical world, though not all biblical writers express it the same way. There is diversity of understandings in this area as in so many areas in the Scriptures. The purposeful nature of God in creating the world is present in Genesis in the first creation account, with its orderly progression of God's dynamic speaking bringing all things into being, step-by-step (Gen 1:1—2:3). Fecundity and flourishing is the divine intent for the world, and human beings are given responsibility for the responsible use and well-being of creation, being made "in the image of God" (Gen 1:27).[4] In this sense, something of the divine purpose is shared with human beings, as is evident in the second Creation account, a sharing that leads to Adam's naming of the animals (Gen 2:19–20) and also the care of the earth: "The LORD God took the man and put him in the garden of Eden to till it and keep it" (Gen 2:15).

The first Creation account uses the language of "dominion" to describe the human participation in God's creation that to our ears, in the context of the ecological crisis, has unfortunate connotations of abuse and exploitation. That indeed is how the Genesis text has been used or rather misused: as "a mandate to violate and dominate all creation."[5] The basic imagery here is both royal and priestly,[6] however, incorporating God's creative work as artisan and ruler of the cosmos, which is shared with human beings: "the divine ruler *delegated* to humans a share in his rule of the earth."[7] Here, God is portrayed as "a generous creator, sharing power with a variety of creatures (especially humanity), inviting them (and trusting them—at some risk) to participate in the creative (and historical) process."[8] This rule, grounded in generosity, love, and freedom, involves the sharing of power with creation.

In the psalms, God's creative rule is evidenced above all in the care and nurture exercised by God. In Psalm 8, the psalmist extols the creation that radiates the glory of its Creator. Like the first Creation account, it sees humankind (however unworthy) as given responsibility for its well-ordering and well-being, under the sovereignty of God (Ps 8:6–8, quoted in Heb 2:6–8 in relation to Jesus). In Psalm 104, it is plain that God's "dominion" signifies God's providential care for creation, providing its security, growth, beauty, and diversity. God enables the earth to produce sufficient food and water to satisfy the needs of all creatures, finally gathering up each one when it departs: "O Lord, how manifold are your works! In wisdom you have made them all; the earth is full of your creatures" (Ps 104:24). Elsewhere, the psalms emphasize that the earth and all its inhabitants belong, not to human beings, but to God (Ps 24:1, quoted in 1 Cor 10:25–26; Ps 50:10–24). This is a God who answers prayer and who is intimately involved in all created life (Ps 65:2).

With the election of God's people and the gift of the promised land, Israel's purpose is to be faithful to the covenant. This theme is dominant in the prophetic writings where covenant loyalty involves two aspects: to worship God and God alone, and to promote God's justice in the land. The fact that God's people fall back again and again into idolatry and social injustice is the perversion of the divine purpose accorded them—though it is never repaid with God's dishonoring of the covenant, even in the expression of judgment. God's purpose is not thwarted but works in and through, even if also sometimes over against, God's people. We have already noted one of the finest expressions of that divinely given purpose: "He has told you, O mortal, what is good; / and what does the Lord require of you / but to do justice, and to love kindness, / and to walk humbly with your God?" (Mic 6:8). True worship leads to acts of justice, with a particular focus on those who are poor and vulnerable. Israel's purpose in worshipping God is thus to protect the poor, a purpose that is perfectly captured by Isaiah:

> The spirit of the Lord God is upon me,
>   because the Lord has anointed me;
> he has sent me to bring good news to the oppressed,
>   to bind up the brokenhearted,
> to proclaim liberty to the captives,
>   and release to the prisoners;
> to proclaim the year of the Lord's favor.
>   (Isa 61:1–2, quoted in Luke 4:18–19)

The New Testament is heir to this tradition and this theology of covenant, rule, love, and justice, by which the guiding purposes of God are expressed. This purpose reaches its climax in the advent of Jesus. As the Beloved Son, Jesus stands in the Old Testament tradition but possesses a sublime identity that makes him ultimately able to restore the whole creation. This purposeful vision of a Savior linked to past, present, and future is summed up in the stately prologue to the Epistle to the Hebrews:

> Long ago God spoke to our ancestors in many and various ways by the prophets, but in these last days he has spoken to us by a Son, whom he appointed heir of all things, through whom he also created the worlds. He is the reflection of God's glory and the exact imprint of God's very being, and he sustains all things by his powerful word. When he had made purification for sins, he sat down at the right hand of the Majesty on high, having become as much superior to angels as the name he has inherited is more excellent than theirs. (Heb 1:1–4)

For the writer of Hebrews, the divine purpose is for God's people to enter into God's rest, with the overthrow of sin and death (Heb 4:1–11); rest is the last act of God's creation on the seventh day (Gen 2:3). This is another way of speaking of the people of God entering into God's beatitude and presence, and thus into intimate communion with God and with one another. By implication, the divine rest is also the destiny of creation, made by God and for God.

The divine purpose is not thwarted by human evil and violence, which are manifest as much in the suffering of creation as in human suffering. Paul links creation's suffering to human failure, presupposing the role and responsibility given to humankind in the Creation accounts. Just as Adam's failure led to the frustration of the purposes of creation, so too will Adam's redemption in Christ restore that purpose.[9] Paul sees the full and final redemption of humankind as having wider implications (Rom 8:19–23), "thereby implying that creation will participate in God's final victory over death."[10] Good will ultimately win out over evil: "We know that all things work together for good for those who love God, who are called according to his purpose" (Rom 8:28). This is a statement of hope that God's benign purpose for believers and indeed for creation itself cannot be overcome by any attempt to thwart it. It finds a medieval parallel in the vision of Julian of Norwich in which Jesus says to her, "All will be well, and all will be well, and all manner of things will be well."[11]

The sense of purpose emerging from the New Testament is fundamentally *God's* purpose into which human beings are drawn: through faith, prayer, and action. They are not simply recipients of divine grace but also participants. Just as they are called in creation to exercise God's beneficent rule over creation, so in God's re-creation they are called to work with God for the renewal of the world. This, in particular, is the purpose and mission of the Church that stands in a unique position, giving hope to the world in its mission:

> With all wisdom and insight [God] has made known to us the mystery of his will, according to his good pleasure that he set forth in Christ, as a plan for the fullness of time, to gather up all things in him, things in heaven and things on earth. (Eph 1:8–10)

The expressed purpose and plan here is that all things are gathered into God's embrace, not just the human world but the whole of creation: "things in heaven and things on earth." It encompasses human history, the life of the Church, all created beings, and all created things. For the writer to the Ephesians, the Christian community has a chosen and privileged role in that divine plan, "created in Christ Jesus for good works" (Eph 2:10). God's purpose gives us purpose, which is ultimately a sharing in the divine purpose rather than importing our own.

It is important, however, not to interpret this sense of divine purpose, in which we are given a share, in a pragmatic or utilitarian way. The ultimate purpose of human life is delight, and delight, above all, in God, who delights in us and in creation. The reiteration of "and God saw that it was good" in the creation narrative (Gen 1:10, 12, 18, 21, 25, 31) illustrates this point beyond any pragmatic sense of purpose. Similarly, in Proverbs, the language of Wisdom, the agent of creation, is that of playfulness and delight as the end goal of the world's existence: "Then I was beside him, like a master worker; / and I was daily his delight, / rejoicing before him always, / rejoicing in his inhabited world / and delighting in the human race" (Prov 8:30–31). Here God's purpose in creating (and therefore redeeming) has its end in joy and pleasure, which parallels the notion of rest in Hebrews:

> It is delight that constitutes creation and so only delight can comprehend it, see it aright, understand its grammar. Only in loving creation's beauty—only in seeing that creation truly is beauty—does one apprehend what creation is.[12]

There is thus both a purposefulness to creation in the biblical world, and also a kind of purposelessness, a sense of a creation born from the creative joy of its God and existing for the pure delight and joy of the Creator and the creatures (Ps 16:11).

READING LUKE ARIGHT

So why might we address this particular set of questions to the Gospel of Luke? After all, Luke is no scientist, nor is he grappling with contemporary questions about the existence of God and the way in which God is, or might be, present to creation. Nor is he attempting to answer philosophical questions about free will and determinism. He does, however, state his purpose at the beginning of his Gospel; he is clear in his carefully worded preface about what he is doing, and his intent has relevance to our concerns in this chapter:

> Since many have undertaken to set down an orderly account [or narrative] of the events that have been fulfilled among us, just as they were handed on to us by those who from the beginning were eyewitnesses and servants of the word, I too decided, after investigating everything carefully from the very first, to write an

orderly account for you, most excellent Theophilus, so that you may know the truth [or assurance] concerning the things about which you have been instructed. (Luke 1:1–4)

Luke is writing with the intention of strengthening faith and providing a solid ground for Christian belief, based in the ministry of Jesus and the events of his life and death. It is this "solid ground for faith" that we are seeking. Not logical proof, however, since Luke uses the word *truth* here to mean "assurance," which implies an inner knowing, a conviction, a sense of faith based on what may or may not be conclusively proven.

As a theologian and storyteller, Luke is deeply concerned about the way God is present in human history, a presence that for him goes back to the origins of Creation. Questions of purpose may not be addressed philosophically or scientifically in this Gospel, but they are addressed in indirect ways through the gospel narrative. And throughout that narrative, Luke explores also the place and significance of prayer in the life of faith.

Before pursuing these themes within the Gospel of Luke, we need first to ensure that we are reading Luke aright, just as we have with the other Gospels. Reading Luke aright means, in the first place, approaching the text in the same way we have approached Matthew's Gospel. We make the assumption that Luke has made extensive use of Mark as the primary Gospel and text with which he has worked.[13] Mark, therefore, would be prominent among the "many" whom Luke tells us have written a narrative of the events of Jesus' life and death—a Gospel, in other words (1:1). Apart from the canonical Gospels, we know little or nothing of any other Gospels written during this period— the second half of the first century. If we are convinced by the view, held by many readers, that Luke is writing independently of Matthew, then we would want to include "Q" in this list, a collection of Jesus' sayings.[14] One thing that Luke makes clear, however, is that he is not himself an eyewitness of the events of Jesus' life and death. Most scholars date him to perhaps the mid-80s, though a later date is also possible.[15]

Luke, however, has made less use of Mark than has Matthew;

even a superficial glance shows that his Gospel differs more from Mark than does Matthew. Luke is also the best and most sophisticated writer among the evangelists, suggesting that he was a well-educated person within the Hellenistic world. His passion for the inclusion of the Gentiles suggests also that he himself was a Gentile; though, if so, he was steeped also in the Old Testament and its writings and traditions. There is no firm tradition of his place of writing, though any Roman-Hellenistic city, where Greek was the common language, would fit. As to his identity, the New Testament speaks elsewhere of "Luke, the beloved physician" (Col 4:14; 2 Tim 4:11; Phlm 24), a companion of John, Mark, and Paul. But Luke was a common name and there is no evidence from the Gospel itself of any specialized medical knowledge on his part. We simply do not know.[16]

In the second place, one thing we do know is that Luke is also responsible for a second volume, the Acts of the Apostles. Though they do not sit side-by-side in the New Testament, Acts makes specific reference to a first volume (Acts 1:1) and there are a large number of parallels between the two texts, including the style of writing and the vocabulary chosen.[17] For our purposes— and for anyone reading Luke's Gospel—we cannot therefore ignore Acts in our study of Luke's Gospel. So, while we may be looking over the fence at the Gospel of Mark, we will equally want to inspect Luke's companion on the other side of the house, a house clearly built by the same architect and in the same style. When we speak of "Luke" therefore, we are primarily focusing on the Gospel of that name, but we have also in mind the Acts of the Apostles.

LUKE AND HISTORY

Luke sees himself as a historian. More than any other evangelist, he is conscious that he is writing history—not history as we might understand it today, but history as it was understood in the ancient world. That means Luke's Gospel is not so much an example of ancient biography—unlike the other Gospels—but rather, along with Acts, an endeavor to produce a history of the

Jesus-movement and the early Church.[18] In that world, the historian might well have an explicit purpose in writing: to teach, to educate, and to inspire virtue in the readers.

As an ancient historian, moreover, Luke's preface includes the claim that he has worked conscientiously in this endeavor. He has engaged in research, as he understands it, consulting other writings of a similar nature and also conversing with the eyewitnesses and the leaders of the Christian community. Oral testimony played a major part in historical research in the ancient world, and the meticulous writer would have spent his time more likely in dialogue with others than in a library.[19] The so-called we-passages in Acts, where Luke suddenly reverts to the first person plural in his narration, suggest Luke's use of written materials as well (Acts 16:11–17; 20:5–15; 21:1–18; 27:1 – 28:16),[20] just as other factors in the third Gospel point to Luke's indebtedness to the Gospel of Mark.

Luke's particular focus on history and the wider political and historical scene becomes apparent to the reader, not only in the preface, but from almost the beginning of the narrative proper. It is already present in the opening reference to King Herod in the story of the annunciation (the angelic announcement) to Zechariah, the first of two annunciations, where the story of John the Baptist's birth parallels that of Jesus (1:5). Similar is the reference to the census and the Roman authorities: the Emperor Augustus and Quirinius, the Roman Governor of Syria.[21]

The fullest expression, however, does not occur till Luke introduces the ministry of John the Baptist, which signals the beginning of Jesus' adult ministry:

> In the fifteenth year of the reign of Emperor Tiberius, when Pontius Pilate was governor of Judea, and Herod was ruler of Galilee, and his brother Philip ruler of the region of Ituraea and Trachonitis, and Lysanias ruler of Abilene, during the high priesthood of Annas and Caiaphas, the word of God came to John son of Zechariah in the wilderness. (3:1–2)

Note that Luke begins with Roman imperial rule across the known world, then the rule of the Herodian family in Palestine, and finally the Jewish leadership in Jerusalem. It commences in Rome and ends in Jerusalem, narrowing down geographically at each point. Luke sets Jesus' ministry in the political context of the Mediterranean world, indicating that he considers the events he will describe to have profound significance in and for that world.[22] In Acts, the Church's ministry will begin in Jerusalem, extending outwards through Judea and Samaria, till it reaches Rome and "the ends of the earth" (Acts 1:8; 28:16).

Luke's historical perspective is generally referred to as "salvation history"—that is, the history of God's salvation in and through Jesus Christ. Luke's two-volume work possesses an "overarching argument" and a "grand narrative that gives meaning to the whole."[23] Its literary shape is constituted by the three phases of God's saving history.[24] The first period is that of Israel, which begins in creation and is grounded in the witness of the Law (Moses) and the prophets (Luke 16:16, 29–31; 24:27, 44). It includes the birth story of Jesus, which commences in Jerusalem with the parents of John the Baptist, moves to Galilee for the annunciation to Mary, and then to Judea and Jerusalem for the births of Jesus and John (1:5—3:1).

The second period is that of Jesus' ministry, life, death, resurrection, and ascension (3:2—24:51). Following Mark's chronology, this period begins with John the Baptist (3:1–18) and covers Jesus' ministry in and around Galilee (3:19—9:50), the transfiguration where Moses and Elijah discuss with Jesus his "exodus"— his departure in Jerusalem (9:28–36)—and Jesus' journey to Jerusalem (9:51—19:28). The travel narrative is much longer in Luke than in Mark and involves additional material relating to mission, teaching, parables, healings, warnings of the future, Jesus' table sharing with sinners, and conflict with the Jerusalem authorities. If there is an element holding this disparate material together, it is the focus on Jerusalem, which is the purpose and goal of the journey (9:51).[25] The central events of salvation take place in and around Jerusalem (Luke 19:29—24:53), where the conflict with the authorities escalates and Jesus is arrested, tried, convicted, and crucified, never losing his trust in God, and dispensing salvation even from the cross. The resurrection appearances likewise take place in and around Jerusalem, as does the story of Jesus' ascension into heaven—a story that both concludes the Gospel and commences the Acts of the Apostles (Luke 24:50–51; Acts 1:9–11).

The third period is the life of the Church and its mission, which occupies the Book of Acts. Just as the Gospel moves toward Jerusalem, as indicated in the birth stories, so in Acts the movement is in the opposite direction, away from Jerusalem.[26] Here, the twelve apostles are reconstituted (with the death of Judas Iscariot, Acts 1:16–26) and, along with Mary, the mother of Jesus, the other holy women, and Jesus' brothers, they receive the gift of the Spirit at Pentecost (Acts 2:1–4). The narrative focuses particularly on the leadership and missionary work of Peter and Paul. The center of Acts, however, is neither of these characters but rather the gospel itself—the message of Jesus Christ, cruci- fied and risen, as the source of salvation—which finally, through persecution and struggle, reaches Rome (Acts 28:14). Like the Gospel, Acts is redolent with the joy of God's good news, direct- ing us to that point where the life and mission of the Church will be fulfilled with the return of Jesus. This event will represent the winding up of history, and the final realization of God's reign (Luke 9:26; 17:30; 21:27; Acts 1:11).[27]

Luke's location of God's story within the wide sweep (as Luke sees it) of history indicates his belief that the divine nar- rative encloses and encompasses the story of Creation. It is the redemption, not just of individuals or even the Christian com- munity, but also of the world. There is, in other words, a definite "world-affirmation" in Luke's Gospel that encompasses not only history but also creation and time; it is a perspective that deals in a kindly way with outsiders and that implicitly values human culture.[28] It demonstrates an "optimistic view of human nature," even a kind of "humanism,"[29] though Luke never for a moment denies the need of salvation.

The point is apparent from the genealogy that Luke pro- vides for Jesus (Luke 3:23–38). The Lukan genealogy differs con- siderably from that of Matthew (Matt 1:1–17).[30] Matthew locates it at the very beginning of his Gospel to introduce the birth story, commencing with Abraham and structuring it in three groups of fourteen generations: Abraham to David, David to the exile, and the exile to Jesus (although Joseph does not actually beget Jesus). Matthew thus sets Jesus exclusively within the story of

112

Israel, even if that story will widen to include Gentiles. By contrast, Luke locates the genealogy after the descent of the Holy Spirit on Jesus and immediately before his ministry begins (Luke 3:21–22). It is therefore directed more at Jesus' ministry than its significance for his birth. Luke's genealogy, moreover, goes backwards, beginning with Joseph and ending, via David and Abraham, with Adam and God. Jesus, in this picture, is "son of God," not just by virtue of his virginal conception but also by his descent from the first "son of God," Adam.[31] Luke traces his genealogy back to Creation itself.

Luke takes an explicitly cosmic view of salvation history, and weds it in the closest possible way to human history and the fate of the cosmos. Jesus' own story goes back to the first human and therefore to the God who created the world and humankind. In that sense, Jesus is in solidarity with every human being and with human history. The salvation that comes from God in Christ (Luke 1:31–35) parallels the creation that also has its source in God. The same God who created humankind now recreates through the history of God's Son. Salvation history represents the possibilities of human history, offered freely by God, just as creation too is the consequence of God's free gift. Luke's cosmic perspective follows his concern for a salvation that has universal scope, in which "all flesh shall see the salvation of God" (3:6; Isa 40:5).[32]

The language that Luke employs across Luke-Acts to designate the salvation manifest in Jesus is indebted both to the Gospel of Mark and to two passages in Isaiah. The notion of the "kingdom of God" as the main focus of Jesus' proclamation is a characteristic feature of the Synoptic Gospels (the phrase appearing only rarely in John).[33] This term has a sense not only of the domain into which we are drawn in Jesus' ministry, but also, and more fundamentally, the sovereign ruling activity of God. Mostly, the word *kingdom* (*basileia*) refers to God's reign (Mark 1:15), but on three occasions it is employed of Jesus' kingdom or reign, a kingdom he is given by the Father (Luke 1:33; 22:30; 23:42). In two contexts, this same kingdom is given to the disciples (12:32; 22:29). It conveys a sense of God's rule as providing the shape and form of human government and human life. In the Lord's Prayer, disciples are to pray for that reign, along with the hallowing of God's name (11:2). God is the final arbiter in human history, and God's reign is the promise of its culmination and salvation.

The other theme that is characteristic of Luke is the verbal form of the phrase "good news" (*euangelizesthai*).[34] This is not an easy verb to translate, as it means literally "to evangelize," and is variously translated "bring good news," "proclaim good news," and "tell good news." The term has its origin particularly in Isaiah 61:1–2, which the Lukan Jesus reads in the synagogue at Nazareth at the beginning of his ministry:

> He unrolled the scroll and found the place where it was written:
>
> "The Spirit of the Lord is upon me,
>   because he has anointed me to *bring good news* to the
>   poor.
> He has sent me to proclaim release to the captives
>   and recovery of sight to the blind, to let the oppressed
>   go free,
> to proclaim the year of the Lord's favor."
>
> …Then he began to say to them, "Today this scripture has been fulfilled in your hearing." (Luke 4:17–19, 21, emphasis added)

Luke uses this passage from Isaiah, along with his conviction of its fulfillment in Jesus, to set the scene for, and summarize the intent of, Jesus' ministry.[35] The other passage from Isaiah is not quoted directly but undergirds Luke's understanding of the good news: "How beautiful upon the mountains / are the feet of the messenger who announces peace, / who brings good news, / who announces salvation, / who says to Zion, 'Your God reigns'" (Isa 52:7). In the Greek version of this text, the verb "evangelize" occurs twice, in reference to the messenger of peace—"the one bringing the message of the good news of peace, the one announcing good things"—and this good news is linked directly to God's kingdom or reign.

For Luke, this proclaiming and bringing of salvation is present

in all the major sections of Luke-Acts. The archangel Gabriel is
the first to bring good news to Zechariah and to the shepherds
(Luke 1:19; 2:10). John the Baptist likewise "proclaimed the good
news" (Luke 3:18) and, most of all, Jesus himself "proclaims [or
brings] the good news of the reign of God" (Luke 4:43), which
is the central feature of his ministry (Luke 7:22; 8:1; 20:1). This
same preaching is given to the disciples whom Jesus sends out
on a mission of proclamation and healing (Luke 9:6; 24:47). Note
that the bringing of good news is not just an oral communication,
but is also made real through action, evidenced especially in concern for the poor, in healing, and in hospitality. Disciples are to
live out their salvation in their commitment to love and justice,
in their hospitality, and in the simplicity of their lifestyle and
sharing of possessions.[36] Through such proclamation in word
and deed, history, for Luke, becomes radiant with the liberating
and restorative good news of God, which is the consequence of
God's saving and merciful reign—with its origins in Israel, its
manifestation above all in Jesus Christ, and its flourishing in the
life of the Church.

LUKE AND PRAYER

In Luke's Gospel, God's beneficence and generosity also
works through the agency of human beings. The story of Mary's
call in the annunciation makes that point clear (1:26–38). Though
a person of no significance in her world, she receives the angelic
message that she is to be the mother of the Messiah: that she is
the chosen vessel, the one empowered by God, the one whose
spirituality has the depth and self-surrender for such a terrifying
vocation. God's generosity in the self-giving of the Son has anything but positive repercussions for Mary, through whose soul a
"sword will pierce" (2:35). Yet Mary responds to the burden of
the divine hospitality with her own generous reply: "Here am
I, the servant of the Lord; let it be with me according to your
word" (1:38). Mary agrees courageously to cooperate with God
in salvation history, despite the consequences to her own life and
reputation, and so becomes the preeminent model of true faith.[37]

Human agency expresses itself in faith and action, directed toward mirroring the divine hospitality and passion for justice.[38] Jesus' ministry reveals the true nature of God, embodying God's own love and being. Disciples are also called to live such a life, committed to the values and practices of the self-revealing God, a call that is fulfilled in the early life of the Church (Acts 2:44–45; 4:32). This cooperation between God and Jesus' disciples is centered on prayer, worship, and mission, which are common themes throughout Luke-Acts.

Luke emphasizes the theme of God working through prayer in his Gospel, as also in Acts.[39] The prayer of the disciples is part of their cooperation with God and God's gracious drawing of them into the divine plan. The theme is clear from the beginning. In the birth narratives, the people of God are at evening prayer when Gabriel appears to Zechariah, who is serving as a priest at the altar of incense (Luke 1:10), and assures him that his prayer and that of his wife for a child has been answered (1:13). The aged widow, Anna, is one who has devoted her whole life to prayer, a prayer that is answered in the birth of the child Jesus (2:37).

Jesus himself exemplifies the life of prayer, and many of the most significant events in the Gospel take place in the context of his prayer. The baptism of Jesus—which Luke, if anything, downplays in comparison to Mark—includes a reference to prayer not found in the other Gospels: "When Jesus also had been baptized and was praying, the heaven was opened, and the Holy Spirit descended upon him in bodily form like a dove. And a voice came from heaven" (Luke 3:21–22). The ascent of prayer here corresponds to the descent of the dove and the voice from above. Later theology speaks of this as a Trinitarian moment in Luke's Gospel—Father, Son, and Holy Spirit—but it should not be forgotten that Jesus also represents the human side. The narrative thus demonstrates not just God's self-revelation, but also the working together of divine and human in and through the power of prayer. In the Lukan Jesus, the cooperation between divine and human is most vividly embodied.

It is the same with the parallel event on the mount of transfiguration. Here too—unlike the other Synoptic Gospels—the dazzling change in Jesus' face and clothing happens in the context of prayer (Luke 9:29). This makes great sense of the transfiguration.

The other two Synoptic Gospels give no reason for Jesus' ascent of the mountain; only Luke indicates that his purpose in going is to pray. What happens next arises, for Luke, from the deepest levels of Jesus' prayer and evokes an immediate response from heaven. The appearance of Moses and Elijah, the overshadowing of the cloud, and the divine voice confirming Jesus' identity and vocation take place in response to his prayerful communion with God (Luke 9:30–35).[40]

These two numinous events, both epiphanies manifesting Jesus' identity and the God who is present to him, are not isolated occurrences in the gospel narrative. On a number of occasions, Jesus retreats from his ministry in order to pray, once to spend an entire night in prayer (Luke 6:12) and once immediately before he first declares his impending passion (9:18). His own prayer is the model and impetus for the Lord's Prayer, which is a shorter version than the Matthean Lord's Prayer, with the disciples asking to be taught how to pray (11:1–4).[41] Jesus also prays for Peter during the passion narrative that he might be both strengthened in his weakness and a source of strength for others (22:32).

In the passion narrative, Jesus prays three times in the context of his suffering, though two of these have textual problems associated with them. He prays at Gethsemane immediately before his arrest (22:39–46), and this prayer is what enables him, through the ordeal, to accede to the will of God and face the cross. In the longer version of this story, Jesus sweats blood and a ministering angel attends him in answer to his prayer. There is also a shorter version, which omits these details of the blood and the angel. The various manuscripts and other witnesses are divided. Whether we choose the longer or shorter text, however, does not detract from the main point, which shows Jesus persisting in prayer and finding the strength to confront his ordeal.

Jesus prays twice from the cross, although there is some doubt as to whether the first of these prayers really belongs. "Father, forgive them; for they do not know what they are doing" (Luke 23:34) is a moving prayer and is most likely part of Luke's original Gospel. It coheres with Luke's emphasis on forgiveness and parallels Stephen's prayer at his martyrdom, where he prays that the sin of his executioners not be held against them (Acts 7:60).[42] Nonetheless, it is absent from an array of early manuscripts. Much more secure within Luke's narrative are Jesus' last words, "Father, into your hands I commend my spirit" (Luke 23:46), which is a quotation from a psalm of lament, expressing the unwavering faith and trust of the righteous sufferer (Ps 31:5).

The words of the penitent thief are, in effect, a prayer addressed to Jesus on the cross: "Jesus, remember me when you come into your kingdom" (Luke 23:42). This prayer for salvation is answered at once by Jesus who assures the man that he will be received at once into heaven. Here the Lukan Jesus not only suffers heroically and trustingly; he also donates salvation from the cross to a sinner. Like the God of this Gospel, the Lukan Jesus responds to prayer with gracious attention and generous benediction. The condemned man is promised his place in Paradise with Jesus.

In this sense, Luke's Jesus also encourages his disciples to pray: at Gethsemane and elsewhere in the Gospel. Luke's version of the Lord's Prayer is followed by Jesus' further teaching on the subject of prayer. Here, the focus is on his encouragement to disciples to bring faith and persistence to prayer, on the basis of the responsive and generous impulse of God (11:5–13). In the Apocalyptic Discourse, where Jesus foretells the future for his disciples, he warns them explicitly to pray (21:36), since being alert to the signs of the times also means being prayerful. Not just any kind of prayer, however; the self-righteous Pharisee of the parable who thanks God for his superiority over others, and especially over sinners, is contrasted with the tax collector who hardly dares to pray and entreats God only for mercy (18:9–14). Jesus assures his hearers that it is the outsider who is justified—whose prayer is heard by God—and not the arrogant insider. For Luke, self-knowing sinners are more open to God and therefore to authentic prayer than the complacent righteous.

The sense of cooperation between divine and human that lies at the heart of Luke's understanding of prayer is similarly emphasized in Acts.[43] The descent of the Spirit at Pentecost takes place while the apostles and the holy women are at prayer (Acts 1:14, 24; 4:31). People are often at prayer when God speaks or acts, sometimes to their astonishment. This occurs with Peter's release from prison for which the Church is praying, though they are astounded when their prayer is answered and refuse at first to

118

believe it (12:5–16). Acts portrays the Holy Spirit working pur-
posefully through all the events that take place, particularly in
the persecution of the Church, and portrays the participation of
the disciples in the spread of the gospel, through their prayer and
openness to the Spirit's guiding presence. It is this focus on the
proximity and power of the Spirit, working in and through prayer,
that is a unifying factor between the Gospel of Luke and Acts.[44]

Finally, we need to make the observation that, while personal prayer is found in Luke-Acts and is strongly encouraged
by the evangelist, the true heart of prayer is the prayer of the
Church. The presence of the apostles in the temple (Acts 3:1–10)
and the gathering together of the early community for prayer
and "the breaking of the bread" make that clear (e.g., Acts
2:42). The same is also true with Jesus teaching the group of
disciples their own particular prayer, which distinguishes them
from other groups who pray (Luke 11:2–4). Prayer, for Luke,
although profoundly personal, is ultimately a companionable
activity.

INTERROGATING LUKE

We have already noted the need to refine the questions we
ask of Luke in regard to divine purpose. The language of "inter-
vention" is unhelpful here, as it suggests a deity who dips a toe
into the human pool from time to time on a whim, or one who
manipulates events and people for obscure ends. Neither of
these statements offers a fair portrait of the God presented by
Luke. Perhaps we might rephrase the question and ask whether
God has a purpose for human history and for the life of creation
and, if so, whether human beings can participate in that purpose.
We might then ask what role is played by our prayers and inter-
cessions, whether they change actual situations, whether they
change God's purpose or God's mind, and how and where in
our lives that purpose is to be found. These resolve themselves
into three questions:

1. Can we speak of a divine purpose for the world and
human history?

2. Do we have a role to play in that purpose?
3. Do our prayers make a difference?

The chances are that the answer to all three questions is a resounding "yes" on Luke's part. But that is not without considerable qualification. We begin with the first question, that of purpose and history. Given his emphasis on salvation history as the cornerstone of his theology in the Gospel and Acts, it would be very difficult to argue that Luke discounts a divine purpose to history.[45] Yet Luke's writings do not suggest that "everything that happens is for a purpose" nor that human beings are manipulated into carrying out God's will in accord with some shadowy, cosmic plan. All through Luke-Acts, people act in accord with their own beliefs, desires, and fears, and from within their own social and religious constructs. Their actions and responses make perfect sense within those constraints.

From one point of view, for example, it is understandable (if regrettable) that the good citizens of Nazareth rise up in rage against Jesus when he commends God's past miraculous attention to needy Gentiles and seeming neglect of similarly situated Israelites (4:25–29). His confronting words strike at the heart of their nationalism and sense of divine privilege. It makes sense politically that Pilate and Herod Antipas should find common ground in their negative response to Jesus at his trial (22:6–16); many a political alliance has been founded in such a mutual opposition. It is understandable that the masters of the slave girl who can foretell the future should be furious with Paul for driving out the demon from her at Philippi, since their source of revenue is now dried up (Acts 16:16–24). Yet none of these characters in their negative response is manipulated by divine providence to respond in the ways they do. God does not provoke them but the reasons for their actions make sense in human and historical terms.

Of course there remains in all this an enigma to what human beings do and say. The question of why, in their respective annunciations, Zechariah doubts the words of Gabriel while Mary does not is not easy to answer (Luke 1:20). Nor does Luke attempt to do so. What emerges, to the reader's surprise, is the picture of an old man, a priest from Jerusalem, showing a less

adequate faith than a young unmarried girl from the backblocks
of Galilee. The same is true, in the broader sweep, in the fact that
Jesus' ministry to sinners and outsiders is markedly more successful than his ministry to the religious authorities (e.g., 15:1–2),
although the two responses are not unconnected. It is Jesus' ministry to those outside the Law that provokes, in part, the hostility
of the jealous guardians of the Law.

The situation with Judas Iscariot is sometimes cited as a
classic example of divine manipulation, with many a Gospel
reader showing sympathy for one caught unwittingly in heavenly machinations. Yet Luke, by contrast, shows no sign of sympathy for Judas and condemns his betrayal of Jesus without
giving reasons for his actions apart from money. It is true that
the apostle Peter, after the ascension, speaks of Judas's actions
as fulfilling the Scriptures (Acts 1:16). At the same time, it is not
the Holy Spirit inspiring the Scriptures who enters into Judas
Iscariot to betray Jesus to the religious authorities, Luke tells us,
but rather Satan, the very embodiment of evil (Luke 22:3).[46] Nor
is this a case of "the devil made me do it," but Luke's way of
showing how Judas, despite his privileged vocation, chooses evil
rather than good. He is certainly not the only human being to
have strayed from the path of goodness to do evil.

To use a rather different and more positive example, it is
entirely natural that Mary rebuke her young son for causing her
and Joseph unspeakable anxiety by staying behind in Jerusalem while they search frantically for him for three days (Luke
2:43–48). Any contemporary mother or father would react in the
same way, foreseeing with dread the beginnings of adolescent
rebellion. But Jesus responds to his parents without rebellion,
sullenness, or apology. Instead he speaks of another identity he
possesses and another parenthood that has even greater claims
upon him. "Why were you searching for me?" he asks them with
some surprise and, "Did you not know that I must be in my
Father's house?" (Luke 2:49)—questions that, not unnaturally,
deprive his parents of speech.

What is happening in this story, the only narrative we have
from Jesus' childhood, is that salvation history is beginning to
gleam out from within the dark folds of human history. There
is another story interacting with the human story of a crisis

between a boy and his parents at a critical stage in his life. Now it becomes also the story of the Son of God responding to his divine Father and his divine vocation, taking his rightful place in the temple, the "house of prayer" (Isa 56:7; Luke 19:46). Yet these two readings are not alternatives. Luke concludes the narrative by noting with approval that the boy Jesus returns home with his parents and is thereafter submissive to their authority. Ordinary human history is hereby resumed, and it is important for Luke that Jesus belongs within that very human context, as well as possessing another, sublime identity.[47]

It is also the case that Jesus speaks of the events of his own suffering, death, and resurrection as enacting the fulfillment of Scripture (Luke 22:37; 24:25–27, 44–47; Acts 2:25–31). Once again, the history of salvation wends its way in and around the ordinary run of human history, neither dominating nor manipulating it. God works with what is and with what people are. Jesus' trial and death make sense within the fallen, human, historical sphere. His passion is the direct consequence of his challenge to the authorities, along with their inability to embrace the radically generous God he proclaims, even to sinners. They prefer instead their own harsh and excluding picture of a God who ensures the maintenance of the status quo.

The resurrection, admittedly, is another proposition entirely. Like the virginal conception, it is an act and an event outside the normal canons of history and history-making: there is no human causality at work here. God alone is responsible for the resurrection, although the human witnesses to this event play a vital role. And God is responsible for Jesus' conception, though only with the cooperation of Mary. The God of Luke's Gospel, in other words, is capable of initiating events beyond the human sphere and particularly where the human story would end only in death and destruction. God brings life out of death, not only, and preeminently, for Jesus but also for his Church. The events of Paul's arrest and trial ensure that the gospel reaches Rome—though God is not responsible for those who oppose Paul's mission and message or for those who sit in judgment on him. They act out of their own freedom and their own choices (Acts 22–26).

God does have a purpose for creation and God's salvation emerges from within human history, with the promise of its ultimate fulfillment: "the last divine activity will correspond to the first—creation."[48] Luke portrays that divine presence as working in and through history to bring life out of death and purpose out of meaninglessness and despair. It is true that in Luke-Acts the sense of a divine purpose is presented in dramatic ways: through healings, dreams, visions, and other miraculous phenomena. But that, in one sense, is Luke's way of underscoring the divine presence continually at work, offering guidance, forgiveness, new life, and the widening of horizons. If our age lacks those obvious signs—or lacks perception of them—this does not discount the divine presence as still operative, still inviting human history and creation to be embraced in God's history, the story of God's saving and life-giving participation in our creaturely story.[49]

This point brings us to our second question, that of participation. Theologically, God does not need our help, hard though it may be for us to realize it. God's own being is entirely self-sufficient. And God, who is also a God of grace and beneficence—a major Lukan theme—also desires to give to each one of us freely, undeservedly, and lovingly. For this reason, and this reason alone, God invites our participation in salvation history. The story of Luke-Acts is, in some respects, the story of those who willingly participate in what God is doing, as well as the story of those who refuse to be involved. All are invited, and Luke is especially aware that the bringing and proclaiming of the good news is not just for God's chosen people, Israel, but for everyone, Gentiles as well as Jews.

There are some whose path of either rejection or welcome is unexpectedly reversed. In the Gospel, as we have seen, Judas Iscariot, one of the chosen Twelve, rejects the divine path. Paul, in Acts, is pursuing the murderous path, which he assumes to be divine, and is brought up short on the Damascus road to confront the One he is really persecuting. Though temporarily blinded by the light, his sight is restored, both literally and figuratively. Paul's story, which he recounts twice more in Acts, turns him from rejection to welcome and to the embrace of suffering in order to tread the divine path (Acts 9:1–9; 22:4–11; 26:12–18). It becomes the story of his participation in salvation history.

We have already noted the exemplary way in which Mary participates in that divine story and the freedom, arising from faith, which causes her to accede to God's word. Theoretically, Mary might have said no to God's demand of her—as the religious authorities do—but her strength of faith and purpose, her belief in the saving Word of God, makes her a particularly appropriate partner in God's salvation. As Elizabeth says of her: "Blessed is she who believed that there would be a fulfilment of what was spoken to her by the Lord" (Luke 1:45).

There are, of course, two ways in which we can speak of our participation in the divine purpose. So far, the focus has been on God choosing us to be partners in salvation history, proclaiming the message of Jesus but also living out that message through mission, service of others, and simplicity of life. The other sense is the more obvious: that God's salvation is aimed at those who need it and those who are aware of their need. Many of the characters in the Gospel and Acts fit into this category, from the man with "the spirit of an unclean demon" who is set free of his suffering (4:33–37), to the centurion whose much-loved slave is dying (7:1–10), to the woman with a severe disability that makes walking upright impossible (13:10–17), and to the lame beggar at the temple gate (Acts 3:1–10).

There is a sense, however, that these suppliants too can be, not only recipients of salvation, but also participants in its dynamic. The leper who is healed is one such person, for he alone of the ten returns to give thanks for his healing (17:11–21). The praise of God is a characteristic theme in the healing stories, revealing that the suppliant has not only been healed in body but also in spirit, and has truly entered the realm of God's reign. "Your faith has saved you/made you well," says Jesus to the leper (who, as an added Lukan touch, is the only one who is a Samaritan), implicitly drawing the man into participation in his own healing (17:21). Another example of this is Mary Magdalene, introduced to us as one who has received an exorcism (8:2), yet who becomes a follower and supporter of Jesus, along with other Galilean women, and a major witness to his death, burial, and resurrection (Luke 24:10).[50] The irony is that Jesus chooses the disabled, the second-class citizens, and the outsiders to proclaim God's liberating and life-giving reign.

The experience of grace that the needy have is the motivation behind their sense of gratitude and desire to extend that reign to others. Luke draws us as readers into the same dynamic. We too are called to be witnesses, in word as well as deed; we too are called to bring the good news to our neighbors, whoever they may be, and to allow our attitudes and structures to be "evangelized." In doing so, however feebly, we are playing our part in God's reign, in God's desire for reconciliation, healing, and wholeness. We, like Jesus himself and the early Church, are to extend the borders of that kingdom beyond the righteous insiders to those on the outside, whether their marginal status is caused by their sin or the sin of others. Welcome, hospitality, forgiveness: these are the signs of God's saving history. And we are drawn into the vocation to exemplify these divine characteristics, allowing God's life-giving purpose to suffuse the particularities of our historical context. Called to "interpret the present time" (Luke 12:56), we are active and intelligent participants in the redemption of history.

As we have seen, prayer is a vital part of the role we are given to cooperate with God in salvation history, because Luke throughout his Gospel "associates prayer with the movement of God's redemptive drama, with gaining or disclosing insight into the reality of that drama and its central character, and with preparation for participation in that same drama."[51]

That means, for Luke, that prayer does make a difference: not just for Jesus and the apostolic community in Luke-Acts but also for us today. We have seen how most of the major events in the Gospel are accompanied by prayer. So too is the shape and form of our ministry and mission, according to Luke. The characteristics of the Church are to include prayer, teaching, the breaking of the bread, the sharing of possessions, mission, the care of the poor, and the sharing of the good news of Jesus' resurrection. These are grounded in Jesus' own ministry, and flow from his and the Church's life of prayer. They point forward to the future coming of Christ:

Just as God has been trustworthy in responding to the diligent prayers of a faithful people in recent history... he will soon grant his chosen ones who perpetually pray their longed-for vindication at the Parousia, having sustained them through every trial.[52]

Luke is clear that prayer makes a difference, not because God is manipulable but rather because that is the way God chooses to work. It is part and parcel of our participation in the bringing, proclaiming, and spreading of the good news. Prayer takes many forms for Luke. But as Church, as disciples, we are to engage in them all: confession of sin, thanksgiving, praise, communion, and petition. It is the last that can give us the most trouble. While some people of faith are happy to petition God, with the expectation of being heard and answered, others find this more difficult and even ambiguous. What about those who do not or cannot pray? Do they miss out? Does God change events as a consequence of our prayers?

There are no definitive answers to these questions; once again, we are up against faith and mystery, not as excuses or rationalizations but as truths beyond our grasp. Luke assures us that God hears our prayers and will respond to them. Yet God does not keep believers out of trouble or save them from pain, tragedy, or persecution. Luke's God is generous and merciful but not a "big Daddy" in the sky to fulfill our every whim or rescue us from every difficulty. God's answers to prayer may be assured but they are not necessarily the answers we might expect. God's answer to Jesus is not the bypassing of the cross but the miracle of the resurrection. Because we do not perceive an answer does not mean that there is none.

As for those who cannot pray, for whatever reason, it is the Church's task to pray on their behalf. This is an essential part of what our cooperation with God in salvation means. The Jesus who departs at the ascension is the one who maintains the closest possible relationship with the world through the coming of the Holy Spirit, who is present to all things and in all things. Jesus himself promises his own return, when the prayers of the saints and the cries of the needy will be fully and finally answered (21:27–28).

We have not so far extended Luke's theology to the needs and cries of a suffering creation, today more than ever before ringing loudly in our ears. Yet within our own context we can discern such a relationship.[53] We ourselves are largely responsible for the dire straits in which the created world now finds itself; it is another aspect of the sin by which we marginalize, ignore, or destroy. It is another indication, too, of our alienation from our Creator and from one another. It is not hard to extend the imperative for social justice in Luke to the realm of creation. Luke, in any case, does not separate creation and human history in the way we do. If salvation history begins with Adam and ends with the return of the Son of Man, then the history of creation is included within its scope. Our participation in God's reign draws our attention to the neighbor—not only the person living literally next door but the one we pass in the street. If Luke can broaden the definition of neighbor to include anyone in need, then it is not too great a step to include also a creation in need.

Twice throughout Luke-Acts, the evangelist shows that creation also experiences suffering in the events leading up to Christ's coming in the last days. Following Mark's Apocalyptic Discourse, Luke outlines the effects on the cosmos:

> There will be signs in the sun, the moon, and the stars, and on the earth distress among nations confused by the roaring of the sea and the waves. People will faint from fear and foreboding of what is coming upon the world [*oikoumenê*], for the powers of the heavens will be shaken. Then they will see "the Son of Man coming in a cloud" with power and great glory. Now when these things begin to take place, stand up and raise your heads, because your redemption is drawing near. (Luke 21:25–28; Dan 7:13)

Luke pictures a kind of cosmic catastrophe, in which all creation and all nations are affected, shaken to their core. Yet Luke's message, for all its emphasis on warning, is ultimately one of hope. His readers are to look up in joyful expectation because their salvation is at hand. It may be that, if our heedless destruction has caused serious damage to the earth, our final liberation will mean also the liberation of creation itself. Shaken though it may be, it is also within the ambit of God's salvation. Once again, the onus lies on us to make effectual the good news of God—over creation as much as over human history. Our prayer, our healing work, and our evangelization are to be directed not only at sinful individuals but also at every aspect of our lives and the life of creation: the structural, political, economic, and environmental aspects of our lives.

CONCLUSION

The meaning we find in our personal lives, which we explored in the Gospel of John, is part of a larger issue that concerns the purpose of human life, and creation as a whole. This issue we have addressed to the Gospel of Luke, the third evangelist. Our questions in this chapter have focused on whether the world is merely a place of random events and chance happenings, or whether it is, in fact, shaped by a sovereign purpose that can give meaning to us, our society and social structures, and to the whole reality of creation. We have addressed these questions with faith, knowing that not every question we ask will find an answer and not every answer will satisfy us.

The Gospel of Luke, along with Acts, its companion volume, implies a strong belief in an ultimate purpose to the world's existence, the key motif being that of salvation history. The Gospel sees human history as shaped definitively by the divine will, without for a moment denying human agency or the efforts of evil to thwart this benign and life-giving purpose. To that end, Luke shapes his account of Jesus' birth and ministry in the wider context of what is, for him, world history. His genealogy of Jesus, as we have seen, goes back beyond Abraham to Adam and thus to creation. Luke calls for our participation and the involvement of creation in God's saving history; here we are both receivers of God's life-giving grace and also, in turn, givers. We participate, above all, through prayer, which flows out into acts of justice and mercy, bringing the good news to bear on our life, in all its dimensions, in both word and deed. Luke strongly affirms a divine, sovereign purpose to history (human history and the history of creation) in which our lives are blessed with redemptive purpose: in the present moment and in the fullness of God's saving time.

It seems appropriate to conclude this discussion on Luke and divine purpose with two prayers: the Collects set down as alternatives for St. Luke's Day (October 18). The first focuses on the healing ministry of Jesus, to be carried over into the life of the Church, a healing that extends to creation. The second focuses on Luke's concern for social justice as integral to salvation, particularly the needs of the poor, with a sense also of Luke's universal focus. Together they capture a sense of Luke's theology of divine purpose in history and creation:

> *Almighty God,*
> *who inspired your servant Luke the physician*
> *to set forth in his gospel the love and healing power of your Son:*
> *graciously continue in your Church this love and power to heal,*
> *to the praise and glory of your name;*
> *through Jesus Christ our Lord,*
> *who lives and reigns with you, in the unity of the Holy Spirit,*
> *one God, now and for ever. Amen.*

> *Gracious and loving God,*
> *you chose Luke the evangelist*
> *to reveal in his gospel the mystery of your love for the poor and*
> *   outcast:*
> *unite in heart and spirit all who profess your name,*
> *and lead all nations to seek your salvation in Jesus Christ, your Son;*
> *who lives and reigns with you and the Holy Spirit,*
> *one God, for ever and ever. Amen.*[54]

Notes

1. John C. Polkinghorne & Nicholas Beale, *Questions of Truth: Fifty-One Responses to Questions about God, Science, and Belief* (Louisville, KY: Westminster John Knox Press, 2009), 15.

2. David Bentley Hart, *The Doors of the Sea: Where Was God in the Tsunami?* (Grand Rapids, MI: Eerdmans, 2005), loc. 571.

3. As Francis Spufford points out, our version of science is itself culturally shaped, "a cultural artifact created by one version of the culture influence of science, specific to the last two centuries….It is not a direct, unmediated picture of reality" (*Unapologetic: Why, Despite Everything, Christianity Can Still Make Surprising Emotional Sense* [London: Faber & Faber, 2012], 144).

4. For an outline of the various theories down through the centuries, see J. Richard Middleton, *The Liberating Image: The Imago Dei in Genesis 1* (Grand Rapids, MI: Brazos Press, 2005), 15–29.

5. Mark Bredin, *The Ecology of the New Testament: Creation, Re-Creation, and the Environment* (Colorado Springs: Biblica Publishing, 2010), 43.

6. See also John Zizioulas (Metropolitan John of Permamon), who argues that the creation stories present an image of humanity as "priest of creation" rather than "proprietor and possessor" of it (John Chryssavgis and Bruce V. Foltz, eds., *Toward an Ecology of Transfiguration: Orthodox Christian Perspectives on Environment, Nature, and Creation* [New York: Fordham University Press, 2013], 163–71).

7. Middleton, *Liberating Image*, 88.

8. Ibid., 296–97, at 271–91.

9. Brendan Byrne, *Romans*, Sacra Pagina 6 (Collegeville, MN: Liturgical Press, 1996), 254–62.

10. Frank J. Matera, *Romans*, Paideia (Grand Rapids, MI: Baker Academic, 2010), 201.

11. See Julian of Norwich, *Revelations of Divine Love* (London: Hodder & Stoughton, 1987), Thirteenth Revelation, chap. 27, p. 55.

12. David Bentley Hart, *The Beauty of the Infinite: The Aesthetics of Christian Truth* (Grand Rapids, MI: Eerdmans, 2003), loc. 3956–67.

13. For an outline of how Luke has used Mark, see Richard Vinson, *Luke*, Smyth and Helwys Bible Commentary (Macon, GA: Smyth & Helwys, 2008), 7–8.

14. The alternative view is that Luke was dependent on Matthew as well as Mark, making use of both in composing his Gospel, thus including Matthew among the "many." See Mark S. Goodacre and Nicholas Perrin, eds., *Questioning Q: A Multidimensional Critique* (London: SPCK, 2004).

15. John T. Carroll sees the range as lying between AD 75 and 125 (*Luke: A Commentary* [Louisville, KY: John Know Westminster, 2012], 3–4).

16. Mikeal C. Parsons, *Luke*, Paideia (Grand Rapids, MI: Baker Academic, 2015), 5–9. For a more extended discussion of

authorship, see Joseph A. Fitzmyer, *The Gospel According to Luke I–IX* (New York: Doubleday, 1979), 35–53.

17. See Robert Tannehill, *The Narrative Unity of Luke-Acts: A Literary Interpretation*, 2 vols. (Minneapolis: Fortress, 1986).

18. Paul J. Achtemeier, Joel B. Green, and Marianne Meye Thompson, *Introducing the New Testament: Its Literature and Theology* (Grand Rapids, MI: Eerdmans, 2001), 62–67. See also Geir O. Holmas, *Prayer and Vindication in Luke-Acts: The Theme of Prayer within the Context of the Legitimating and Edifying Objective of the Lukan Narrative*, The Library of New Testament Studies (London: Bloomsbury, 2011), 49–58.

19. On this point and on Luke's preface, see Richard Bauckham, *Jesus and the Eyewitnesses: The Gospels as Eyewitness Testimony* (Grand Rapids, MI: Eerdmans, 2006), 114–47.

20. Is it unclear whether these passages come from Luke's own participation in the events or from a source he is quoting more directly; see Parsons, *Luke*, 5–7.

21. The problem is that Quirinius held the position from AD 6–12 when Herod the Great was already ten years dead. Jesus most likely was born around 4 BC. See Raymond E. Brown, *The Birth of the Messiah: A Commentary on the Infancy Narratives in Matthew and Luke* (New York: Doubleday, 1979), 547–56.

22. On the leading figures mentioned here, see Darrell L. Bock, *Luke 1:1 — 9:50*, ECNT (Grand Rapids, MI: Baker Academic, 1994), 279–84.

23. Justo L. González, *Luke*, Belief: A Theological Commentary on the Bible (Louisville, KY: Westminster John Knox, 2010), 3.

24. Fitzmyer, *Luke I–IX*, 179–92.

25. Luke Timothy Johnson, *The Gospel of Luke*, Sacra Pagina 3 (Collegeville, MN: Liturgical Press, 1991), 161–65. For an overview of the journey, see Joel B. Green, *The Gospel of Luke*, NICNT (Grand Rapids, MI: Eerdmans, 1997), 394–99.

26. Johnson, *Gospel of Luke*, 14–15. Unlike Mark and Matthew (and John 21), Luke records no appearances of the risen Christ in Galilee; everything for him is centered on Jerusalem.

27. Fitzmyer, *Luke I–IX*, 185; also Brendan Byrne, *The Hospitality of God: A Reading of Luke's Gospel* (Collegeville, MN: St. Paul's, 1989), 14–16.

28. Johnson, *Gospel of Luke*, 21–22.

29. François Bovon, *A Commentary on the Gospel of Luke*, Hermeneia (Minneapolis: Fortress, 2002), 1:11.

30. Brown, *Birth of the Messiah*, 84–94.

31. González, *Luke*, 54–56.

32. Green, *Gospel of Luke*, 394–95.

33. Vinson, *Luke*, 10–12.

34. Johnson, *Gospel of Luke*, 33.

35. The quotation includes a reference to the Year of Jubilees—the year of "release"—that was to occur in the fiftieth year and during which the land was to lie fallow, all indentured Israelites were to be set free, and land sold returned to its owners (Lev 25). On this and on the relationship of Luke's text to the original in Isaiah, see Byrne, *Hospitality*, 46–50.

36. Christopher M. Tuckett, *Luke* (Sheffield: Sheffield Academic Press, 1996), 94–110; and Carroll, *Luke*, 374–77.

37. Vinson, *Luke*, 34–40.

38. Byrne, *Hospitality*, 4–5.

39. Holmas, *Prayer and Vindication*, 58–61, 63–155; and Wilfrid J. Harrington, *Reading Luke for the First Time* (Mahwah, NJ: Paulist Press, 2015), 137–60.

40. Dorothy A. Lee, *Transfiguration*, New Century Theology (London: Continuum, 2004), 65–87.

41. See Carroll, *Luke*, 249–53.

42. See Bovon, *Luke*, 3:306–7; and Carroll, *Luke*, 464–66.

43. See Holmas, *Prayer and Vindication*, 157–260.

44. Tannehill, *Narrative Unity of Luke-Acts*, 1:237–40.

45. For a summary of this theme in Lukan commentators, see François Bovon, *Luke the Theologian: Fifty-Five Years of Research (1950–2005)* (Waco: Baylor University Press, 2006), esp. 13–82.

46. Robert C. Tannehill, *Luke*, ANTC (Nashville: Abingdon Press, 1996), 310–11.

47. Vinson, *Luke*, 74–79.

48. Bovon, *Luke the Theologian*, 85.

49. On the *missio Dei* (mission of God) as extending to all of creation, see Dianne Bergant, "*Missio Dei*: The Transfiguration of All Creation," in *Where the Wild Ox Roams*, ed. Alan H. Cadwallader and Peter L. Trudinger (Sheffield: Phoenix Press, 2013), 86–100.

50. See Esther A. de Boer, "The Lukan Mary Magdalene and

the Other Women Following Jesus," in *A Feminist Companion to Luke*, ed. Amy-Jill Levine (Cleveland: Pilgrim Press, 2001), 140–60.

51. Craig G. Bartholomew and Robby Holt, "Prayer in/and the Drama of Redemption in Luke: Prayer and Exegetical Performance," in *Reading Luke: Interpretation, Reflection, Formation*, eds. Craig G. Bartholomew, Joel B. Green, and Anthony C. Thiselton, Scripture and Hermeneutics 6 (Grand Rapids, MI: Zondervan, 2005), 357.

52. Holmas, *Prayer and Vindication*, 266.

53. For an excellent summary of Luke's concern with creation, see David Rhoads, "Overall Care for Creation: Reflections on the Gospel of Luke in Year C for Preaching and Devotion," http://www.lutheransrestoringcreation.org/overall-care-for-creation-reflections-on-the-gospel-of-luke-in-year-c-for-preaching-and-devotion.

54. *A Prayer Book for Australia* (Melbourne: Broughton Publishing, 1995), 620.

CONCLUSION

We have focused on the Gospels on the grounds that they contain considerable wealth of meaning—enough to address our questions to them and hope for significant and even profound answers. Other questions remain unanswered and may even be unanswerable. The focus of this study has been narrow, in one sense, but it has given us the opportunity to explore the Gospels through a single lens. It has also enabled us to explore each gospel narrative as a whole and gain some sense of its direction and meaning. In each case, a contemporary issue or concern has been addressed to a single Gospel, and explored for its resources and insights.

We began with the Gospel of Mark—the first Gospel to be written—and examined what it might have to say to us about suffering, sin, evil, and death. In the passion and death of Jesus, which is so central a theme in this Gospel, God enters into the depths of human suffering—our pain and abandonment—identifying with them to the full. Out of the depths of our sin and suffering, which Jesus embraces on the cross, emerges the resurrection: the empty tomb, the angelic visitor, and the promise of Christ's appearance in Galilee. Mark combines a focus on suffering, and a suffering Messiah, with his apocalyptic vision, and his belief in the final triumph of God and of God's reign, to be made visible in the future coming of the Son of Man, the same Son of Man who was also crucified. Suffering and triumph are the great twin themes of Mark's Gospel.

Turning next to the Gospel of Matthew—most likely the next Gospel in chronological order and dependent on Mark's narrative for its structure and contents—we explored issues of fear and anxiety, and how Matthew responds to these, especially when they are chronic or overwhelming. Fear in our world is growing and anxiety is a major problem in many lives, often linked to mental illness. Even without such diagnosis, there are people—even of religious faith—who live lives that are shrouded in anxiety and dread.

Matthew, as we saw, depicts fear in vivid ways through both narrative and discourse. Not all fear is negative in the biblical world—the fear of God is a way of speaking of the awe that God's beauty and majesty call forth in all mortal beings. Yet Matthew is aware of other kinds of fear that are life-denying and crippling. Jesus calms the disciples' fear on several occasions, but also speaks overtly in the Sermon on the Mount about the need to live in trust and without worry or anxiety. Matthew's spirituality involves a deep belief, touching heart as well as head, in the providential goodness and generosity of God. Meditation is one way in which we can experience that trust and move beyond anxiety.

It may have seemed more logical to move directly to the Gospel of Luke, as the third of the Synoptic Gospels, but it was also appropriate to commence our last two related questions with the more personal (John) before concluding with the cosmic (Luke). It is also important to set the Gospel of Luke alongside the Acts of the Apostles, Luke's second volume; it is impossible to speak of one without reference to the other.

With John, the issue was that of personal meaning and longing. Here, the focus was different from that in previous chapters, where the Gospels themselves spoke overtly of the issue under discussion: Mark has much to say about suffering, as does Matthew about fear and anxiety. The conception of meaning, however, is not explicit in John—no such language appears—and so our question was one that, at a certain level, lay beyond the text. However, unpacking the Johannine narrative, we saw that, while the language itself might be absent, similar concepts are present. John's notion of eternal life, wending its way through the gospel narrative, includes by implication the notion of meaning. In all the richness of the life that Jesus brings, in the sense of joy and peace and the experience of truth and love, John offers meaning to human life, a meaning that enriches the present and that cannot be overcome by death. John's understanding of discipleship, in the various images employed, conveys a profound sense of meaning in living, both in the future and the here-and-now, a meaning that transcends death. John also addresses the human longing for authentic life, a longing that is ultimately fulfilled in relationship with God through Jesus, who is the Way to God, the Truth about God, and the Life of God. Questions of meaning and longing are intricately linked and both find an appealing answer in the narrative and symbolism of the Fourth Gospel.

Finally, the question of purpose seemed particularly apt for the Gospel of Luke, with its strong focus on salvation history and its implicit concern for all that God has made. For Luke, God is operating within the world in order to transform it, offering an alternative narrative to that of "secular" space and time, yet one that wends its way in and around the events of history and creation. Luke's strong sense of a divine purpose implies, not the lessening of human freedom and choice, but rather its confirmation. Luke sees human participation, if freely given, as essential to God's plan of salvation—not because God needs us but because God graciously chooses to work in us and through us. This sense of purpose and participation implies, in particular, a role for prayer, and Luke demonstrates the conviction that God works through prayer and responds to the cries of the poor and needy—though not always in ways we might expect.

But what of the other Gospels not covered by each of our questions? Might they too not have something to say on the same issues? Is their voice to be confined to the one question alone? In this conclusion, it is worth looking again at the core questions and observing briefly what each of the other Gospels might reveal.

SUFFERING AND EVIL (MATTHEW, LUKE, AND JOHN)

While the Gospel of Mark may have the greatest focus on suffering, all the Gospels have something to say about evil, sin, suffering, and death. All four record Jesus' ministry of alleviating suffering through his ministry of healing, his confrontation with evil, and his raising of the dead. For Matthew, Jesus' healing ministry accompanies his teaching ministry, revealing him to be the true Messiah, authentic in word and deed. Jesus' response to the question of John the Baptist from prison follows the Sermon on the Mount (Matt 5:1—7:1) and the healing actions (Matt 7:2—9:38), a dual ministry that is then handed on to the disciples (Matt 10:1–42). On this basis, Jesus can answer a resounding yes to the Baptist's question (Matt 11:2–5); he has indeed healed and proclaimed good news.[1] Only Jesus has the capacity in this way to remove suffering: "He took our infirmities and bore our diseases" (Matt 8:17; Isa 53:4).[2]

Like Matthew, Luke also follows many of Mark's miracle stories, emphasizing that Jesus' coming is to alleviate human misery and overcome the forces of evil that captivate and confine human life (Luke 4:16–21): healing, exorcizing demons, and raising the dead. For Luke, such misery includes poverty and injustice, and the coming reign of God involves a reversal in which God is seen to have "brought down the powerful from their thrones, and lifted up the lowly" (Luke 1:52; see 6:20–26).[3] This reversal is apparent in the way in which "sinners" are drawn toward Jesus and into the hospitality of God embodied in his ministry, while the religious leaders are increasingly alienated by Jesus' inclusive and emancipatory agenda (Luke 15:1–2).[4] The mood of joy and praise that suffuses Luke is the expression of buoyant gratitude for God's life-giving and liberating power, triumphing over sin, tragedy, injustice, and exclusion, and finally death itself (Luke 2:10; 24:52).

John's Gospel differs from the Synoptics in that he includes no exorcisms in his narration of Jesus' ministry. His focus, though, in one sense apocalyptic,[5] is much more concerned with the "now" of Jesus' presence and its capacity to transform the present moment ("I *am* the resurrection and the life," John 11:25, emphasis added), in long narratives often focused on an individual. The "signs" of the ministry have a distinctly theological flavor, not just alleviating physical suffering but also spiritual suffering, apparent in the revelation of Jesus' divine glory (John 2:11): feeding the hungry as the Bread of life (John 6:1–35), offering the thirsty the living water of the Spirit (John 7:37–39), and illuminating blind eyes as the Light of the world (John 9:1–7).[6]

All four Gospels focus centrally on the cross and the suffering of Jesus, interpreting it paradoxically as an enthronement where Jesus' true sovereignty is ironically revealed.[7] It is true that none has the same focus on Jesus' abjection and powerlessness as Mark. Matthew's Jesus remains firmly in control of events (Matt 26:53), Luke's Jesus dies with the calmness of trust in his God (Luke 23:46), while for John, the cross represents the revelation of the divine glory and the divine love for the world (John 3:16–17; 13:1, 31–32; 19:30). In each case, however, there is a sense of triumph achieved through suffering—triumph over all that is evil, unjust, life-denying, alienating, and deathly sinful. The divine victory occurs in and through the cross for each evangelist, challenging the powers of evil and the dominating and oppressive ways they operate in the world.

FEAR AND ANXIETY (LUKE, MARK, AND JOHN)

The concern to allay fear and anxiety is a feature of the Gospel of Luke as well as Matthew, a Gospel that shares many of the same sayings that relate to this theme (e.g., Luke 12:22–31). For Luke, disciples are also encouraged to live without anxiety, secure in the knowledge of the Father's protective love that extends to all creation (Luke 12:6–7). What is to be feared, however, are the forces of evil and destruction (12:5). Yet even here Jesus assures his disciples, following the mission of the seventy, that Satan has already been overcome: "I watched Satan fall from heaven like a flash of lightning. See, I have given you authority to tread on snakes and scorpions, and over all the power of the enemy; and nothing will hurt you" (Luke 10:18–19).[8] For Luke, the reason disciples do not have to fear is that the powers ranged against God have already been toppled and the kingdom assured (Luke 12:32).

Fear is also a theme in Mark's Gospel, and at several points the disciples are encouraged not to be afraid or alarmed, including the women disciples at the empty tomb (Mark 5:36; 6:50; 13:7;

139

16:6). Whether this message is heeded is another question; many of the disciples, particularly the inner group, do not fare particularly well in Mark's narrative.[9] Mark sees fear as the opposite of faith (Mark 4:40), and faith itself as a gift, a miracle of perception and understanding that takes time to grasp. On the road to Jerusalem, the disciples do not manage to overcome their fear as they follow Jesus on his cross-bearing journey (Mark 10:32), but understanding is given to those who need it and request it. Significantly, the journey is bounded by two stories of the healing of blind eyes (Mark 8:22–26; 10:46–52). What the disciples lack in fear is made up for in the risen Christ's continued leading of his frail disciples and in his gift of understanding.[10]

The theme of giftedness in the face of fear is also present in John's Gospel. In the Farewell Discourse, one of the great gifts Jesus gives his sorrowing disciples is that of peace: "Peace I leave with you; my peace I give to you. I do not give to you as the world gives. Do not let your hearts be troubled, and do not let them be afraid" (John 14:27). Fear, for John, is inevitable given the hostility of the unbelieving world toward truth and goodness (e.g., John 9:22; 19:38), and the disciples will suffer as a consequence. Their confidence, however, lies not in their own capacity but in the fact this same "world" has been overcome (John 16:33).[11] Whatever they experience in the way of suffering is temporal and temporary, and not part of God's final reality. Indeed, the fate of evil and suffering is already sealed through Jesus' incarnation and death. Among his final words to his disciples, following his resurrection on Easter Day, is the gift of his peace (John 20:19, 21).[12]

MEANING (MARK, MATTHEW, AND LUKE)

The theme of meaning and its accompanying motif of longing (which as we have already seen, is not explicit in the Gospel of John) is present in a similarly implicit or hidden way in the other Gospels. As with John, discipleship confers a deep meaning on human life beyond the everyday. Indeed, for the

Synoptic Gospels, the meaning to be gained in relationship with Jesus may well entail the surrender of other human goods and values for its sake. Matthew speaks, for example, of those who have embraced a life of celibacy, refusing the joys and security of marriage and family: "eunuchs for the sake of the kingdom of heaven" (Matt 19:12).[13] Luke in particular emphasizes this theme, with his attitude to wealth and poverty and his sense that, for the followers of Jesus, discipleship involves the sharing of possessions, since possessions stand far from the center of true meaning: "One's life does not consist in the abundance of possessions" (Luke 12:15).[14]

The Synoptic theme of a deeper meaning to be found in following Jesus is present particularly in the story of the wealthy man who approaches Jesus (Mark 10:17–27; Matt 19:16–22; Luke 18:18–27). The man, described as "young" in Matthew and as a "ruler" in Luke (and therefore a man of considerable status), is one who feels his life, despite its prosperity and propriety, to be seriously lacking. The question of eternal life does not just concern his fate for the future beyond death. It contains a sense also that something needs to happen in the present moment that is not happening; something needs to be done that the man is not doing. He comes to Jesus as to a wise teacher, who might help fill the bewildering emptiness of his life.

Jesus' answer comes as a shock, both to the man himself and to the disciples. The summons to surrender his possessions and donate them to the poor, thereby becoming a travelling companion of Jesus and committed to a life of evangelical poverty, is beyond the man's comprehension or his desires. He does not see it as a liberating honor that is given to the few (the Twelve and the holy women, Luke 8:1–3), but as a terrifying burden. In all three Gospels, Jesus identifies the void in the man's life, pinpointing the precise obstacle to his salvation, the very thing preventing him from finding authentic meaning in his life, and offering him instead a privileged vocation.[15] Mark tells us that Jesus loved the rich man, a detail omitted from Matthew and Luke, but in any case the man turns away grieving (Mark 10:21–22; Matt 19:22) and sad (Luke 18:23). The cost is too high; the longing not sufficiently strong for what is asked of him.[16]

At the end of the story, Jesus assures his disciples that what stands outside the human capacity to achieve—the surrender of wealth for the sake of the kingdom—lies within the gift and provenance of God: "For mortals it is impossible, but not for God; for God all things are possible" (Mark 10:27). Here, the notion is one of costly grace, a grace that is freely bestowed but potentially costs the disciple everything. Meaning is not to be found under every bush and stone; its discovery is rare and precious, and it demands all of those who seek it. This theme is powerfully present in two parallel Matthean parables of the Treasure and the Pearl (Matt 13:44–46). In the first, the treasure is found by accident, and in the second, the pearl has been long sought; but in both cases, the main character sells everything for the priceless gift. Meaning makes its own demands for the Synoptic evangelists.

Peter's final response after the departure of the wealthy man reveals, however, that renunciation has its own rewards: "Truly I tell you, there is no one who has left house or brothers or sisters or mother or father or children or fields, for my sake and for the sake of the good news, who will not receive a hundredfold now in this age—houses, brothers and sisters, mothers and children, and fields with persecutions—and in the age to come eternal life" (Mark 10:29–30; also Matt 19:29; Luke 18:30). These benefits represent far more than mere compensations. They signify the finding of true meaning and life, both in the immediate sense—the discovery of an equivalent sense of family and belonging—and in the age to come. What the disciples have discovered as meaningful is, in fact, an enduring treasure that survives and thrives on the other side of death, satisfying completely the longing for authentic life: a profound connection to God's gracious, sovereign rule.

PURPOSE (MARK, MATTHEW, AND JOHN)

Luke is renowned for his emphasis on a theology of salvation history, as we have seen, a theology that is not given the same emphasis or shape in the other Gospels. Each of them possesses, however, a sense of a cosmic, divine purpose for human life and creation. This purpose, as with Luke, is centered on Jesus of Nazareth and on the events of his life, ministry, death, and resurrection. Admittedly, the Synoptic expression of this cosmic vision is very different from the Johannine version, but all the Gospels exhibit a vivid and pervading awareness of God radically at work in Jesus and in the life of the Church, to transform the world and its inhabitants. These Gospels reveal a portentous sense of universal purpose.

Thus, for example, in addition to the broad schema of the gospel and a similar cast of characters and events, Matthew and Mark share an overtly apocalyptic perspective on the Christ event. Their focus is on the destiny of the world as the divine future stretches back in time and begins already to reform and reshape the present. Jesus walks onto the stage in both Gospels to proclaim the nearness of God's final, apocalyptic reign: a reign of goodness, justice, and love that will ultimately prevail (Mark 1:14–15; Matt 4:17).

Influenced by the apocalyptic writings in the second half of the Book of Daniel (7–12) and later Jewish apocalyptic literature, this perspective is, by definition, cosmic. Though it deals with the trials and tribulations of the small, elect community of God's people, it sets their experience within the universal sphere of God's ultimate triumph over the forces of evil. Not only the nations of the earth, but also the terrestrial and celestial spheres are profoundly affected by the Jesus event and drawn into its dynamic (Mark 13:24–25; Matt 24:29). This apocalyptic emphasis is already prefigured in the events of the crucifixion, which likewise shake the cosmic sphere (the three-hour darkness, the tearing of the temple veil, and the earthquake: Mark 15:33–38; Matt 27:45–53). God's future purpose for the world is assured in this apocalyptic vision.

We have already observed that John's Gospel stresses the present rather than the future as the sphere of God's saving activity. For John, it still remains in God's future but its reality is largely, though not exclusively, anticipated in the present. Jesus says to Thomas, "Blessed are those who have not seen and yet have come to believe" (John 20:29), implying that the readers of the Gospel, wherever and whenever they exist, have the same access to Christ as the original apostolic community: Mary Magdalene and Thomas, Simon Peter and the Beloved Disciple. They have the same access to the risen Christ through the Holy Spirit whom Jesus breathes on them, making real for believers the presence of the absent Jesus (John 20:22).

John's cosmic vision is unveiled in the Prologue of the Gospel, where the Word who existed with God from before creation, and through whom the world was created, is the one who also becomes flesh (John 1:1–3, 14). In the incarnation, Creator becomes creation; the one who signifies "being" enters the world of "becoming"; the eternal becomes temporal. This is by definition a cosmic event: it is the same Creator God acting through the same Word/word who now purposes to redeem the world by taking on the world's being, including its hatred, rejection, and violence. This redemption is not just for human beings but for all that is implied by the term *flesh*, suggesting creation as a whole. The same phrase that is repeated in Jesus' Great Prayer which literally translates, "Since you have given him authority over *all flesh*, to give eternal life to all that you have given him" (John 17:2).[17] The world as the object of the Father's purpose to save and not condemn (John 3:16–17) is the domain of both creation and redemption: the one realm of God's creative and restorative love.

Prayer in these Gospels is likewise a participation in God's saving purpose. In each Gospel, Jesus himself is a person of prayer and draws others into his prayer. In Matthew's Gospel, the Lord's Prayer, the model of all true prayer, stands at the heart of the Sermon on the Mount, invoking the spirituality that lies behind Matthew's ethics (Matt 6:9–13). To pray this prayer is to be drawn into the dynamic of the kingdom of heaven, to seek it and strive for it above all else (Matt 6:33). This orientation toward the coming kingdom shapes the prayer and therefore the future hopes and the present lives of disciples.[18] Like Jesus, they too are to be people of prayer, a community of prayer and mission in which they orient their lives toward God's final kingdom.

John's concept of participation goes further. Disciples are drawn into Jesus' own prayer and therefore into union with him and with the Father, as well as with one another (John 17:21). They participate in eternal life—the Johannine equivalent of the

Synoptic kingdom of God/heaven—not so much as an external gift but rather in the context of relationship. Because they are gathered up into Jesus' prayer, they enter into his filiation, his identity as the Son, and so become sons and daughters of God, their original, created identity now restored.[19] They are sent out on the Father's mission by the Son in the power of the Spirit (John 20:21).

The other three Gospels, in other words, also project the sense of a divine purpose in creation, a purpose that is not thwarted by sin and evil but rather breaks through the barriers to open up the way to God—not just for human beings but for the whole creation.[20] The same Gospels also include the community of disciples in that saving purpose, an inclusion that involves them in prayer, as also in mission. For Matthew, it is Jesus' prayer that teaches us how to pray with our eyes on God's future reign. For John, we are included in Jesus' prayer to the Father and thus enfolded into the intimacy of his relationship with God and the assurance of his saving purpose for the world.

POSTSCRIPT

We read the Bible as part of a centuries-long dialogue between its own diverse and untidy contents and the ever-changing questions and needs of our own cultures. We talk and we listen, studying to speak coherently and struggling to hear voices that echo dimly and darkly down the long corridors of time. Perhaps we gain a sense of what might happen if we were to address the same questions to other biblical texts: to Paul and Hebrews, to James and Revelation, to Genesis and Isaiah, to Ruth and Malachi. The main point is that the Bible, for all that, belongs in an ancient and alien culture, far behind us in space and time, yet still has the remarkable capacity to speak to us today across the centuries. To ask questions of this ancient text, in all its diversity, means respecting its otherness, its difference from us, the complexities of its context and ways of thinking and writing. But the hard work required of us for this enterprise is well worthwhile. The Bible has much to say to our deepest human needs and longings—not as isolated verses taken out of context, but in its overall narrative and rhetoric. Each example of biblical theology from across the wealth and breadth of Scripture has its own answer to offer if we only know how to ask and therefore to receive.

NOTES

1. Donald A. Hagner, *Matthew 1–13*, World Biblical Commentary 33A (Nashville: Thomas Nelson, 2000), 195–96, 300–301.

2. The sense is not so much Jesus' vicarious suffering on the cross, but rather his healing ministry: "he took *away* our infirmities and *bore off* our diseases." Overall, however, Matthew does have a sense of the cross as vicarious, in keeping with the quotation from Isaiah. See W. D. Davies and Dale C. Allison, *Matthew: A Shorter Commentary* (London: T & T Clark, 2004), 124, and Craig S. Keener, *The Gospel of John: A Commentary* (Peabody: Hendrickson, 2003), 273.

3. Joel B. Green, *The Gospel of Luke*, NICNT (Grand Rapids, MI: Eerdmans, 1997), 263–68.

4. Brendan Byrne, *The Hospitality of God: A Reading of Luke's Gospel* (Collegeville, MN: Liturgical Press, 1989), 4–5.

5. On the way in which John can be said to be apocalyptic, see John Ashton, *Understanding the Fourth Gospel* (Oxford: Clarendon, 1991), 283–406.

6. Dorothy A. Lee, *Flesh and Glory: Symbol, Gender and Theology in the Gospel of John* (New York: Crossroad, 2002), 36–45.

7. See, for example, Robert Kysar, *John: The Maverick Gospel* (Louisville: Westminster John Knox, 2007), 60–66.

8. Arthur A. Just, *Luke 9:51–24:53* (St. Louis: Concordia Publishing House, 1997), 443–44.

9. On the various complex groupings in Mark's Gospel, including the disciples and the Twelve, see M. Eugene Boring, *Mark: A Commentary*, New Testament Library (Louisville: Westminster John Knox, 2006), 167–70.

10. See Francis J. Moloney, who takes the view that the

women disciples fail at 16:8 along with the other disciples. *The Gospel of Mark: A Commentary* (Peabody: Hendrickson, 2002), 352–54.

11. "In the midst of conflict and persecution his followers can know an ultimate security that is an antidote to fear" (Andrew T. Lincoln, *The Gospel According to Saint John*, Black's New Testament Commentary [London: Continuum, 2005], 397).

12. Interestingly, in 1 John, the opposite of love is not only hatred but also fear, in this case probably fear of judgment (1 John 4:18–19); see Dorothy A. Lee, *Hallowed in Truth and Love: Spirituality in the Johannine Literature* (Melbourne/Eugene, OR: Mosaic/Wipf & Stock, 2011–12), 210.

13. On the radical nature of the metaphor, see Keener, *Gospel of Matthew*, 471–72.

14. For Luke, disciples "do not live in a world of chaotic chance, but in a world governed by the gracious gift of God. Only because they have been so fundamentally gifted can they be without fear and therefore can share their possessions with others" (Luke Timothy Johnson, *The Gospel of Luke*, Sacra Pagina 3 [Collegeville, MN: Liturgical Press, 1991], 202).

15. In a parallel passage from Luke, Jesus informs Martha that "there is need of only one thing" (Luke 10:42); see Arthur A. Just, *Luke 9:51–24:53* (St. Louis: Concordia Publishing House, 1997), 697.

16. Note the various exegetical attempts down through the centuries to tone down the radical demands of this passage: Boring, *Mark*, 291–93.

17. For some reason, the NRSV chooses to paraphrase the Greek here, losing the sense of a wider domain for salvation and confining it to humankind: "Since you have given him authority over all people, to give eternal life to all whom you have given him"; see Lee, *Flesh and Glory*, 43–45.

18. Davies and Allison, *Matthew*, 90–96.

19. Lee, *Hallowed in Truth and Love*, 149–50.

20. The verb Mark uses at the baptism of Jesus is telling: Jesus "saw the heavens *torn apart* and the Spirit descending like a dove on him" (1:10). The same verb is used in Mark of the tearing of the temple curtain at the crucifixion (15:38), with its background in Isa 64:1 ("O that you would tear open the heavens and come down…"); Boring, *Mark*, 45.

BIBLIOGRAPHY

Achtemeier, Paul J., Joel B. Green, Marianne M. Thompson. *Introducing the New Testament: Its Literature and Theology*. Grand Rapids, MI: Eerdmans, 2001.

Alexander, Loveday. "Ancient Book Production and the Circulation of the Gospels." In *The Gospels for All Christians: Rethinking the Gospel Audiences*, edited by Richard Bauckham, 71–111. Edinburgh: T & T Clark, 1998.

Allison, Dale C. *The New Moses: A Matthean Typology*. Minneapolis: Fortress, 1993.

Anderson, Paul N. *The Fourth Gospel and the Quest for Jesus: Modern Foundations Reconsidered*. London: T & T Clark, 2006.

Barrett, C. K. *The Gospel According to St John*. 2nd ed. London: SPCK, 1978.

Bartholomew, Craig G., and Robby Holt. "Prayer in/and the Drama of Redemption in Luke: Prayer and Exegetical Performance." In *Reading Luke: Interpretation, Reflection, Formation*, edited by Craig G. Bartholomew, Joel B. Green, and Anthony C. Thiselton, 350–75. Grand Rapids, MI: Zondervan, 2005.

Bauckham, Richard, ed. *The Gospels for All Christians: Rethinking the Gospel Audiences*. Edinburgh: T & T Clark, 1998.

———. *Jesus and the Eyewitnesses: The Gospels as Eyewitness Testimony*. Grand Rapids, MI: Eerdmans, 2006.

———. *The Testimony of the Beloved Disciple: Narrative, History, and Theology in the Gospel of John*. Grand Rapids, MI: Baker Academic, 2007.

Bergant, Dianne. "*Missio Dei*: The Transfiguration of All Creation" In *Where the Wild Ox Roams*, edited by Alan H. Cadwallader and Peter L. Trudinger, 86–100. Sheffield: Phoenix Press, 2013.

de Boer, Esther A. "The Lukan Mary Magdalene and the Other Women Following Jesus." In *A Feminist Companion to Luke*, edited by Amy-Jill Levine, 140–60. Cleveland: Pilgrim Press, 2001.

Boring, M. Eugene. *Mark: A Commentary*. Louisville, KY: Westminster John Knox, 2006.

Bovon, François. *A Commentary on the Gospel of Luke*. 3 vols. Hermeneia. Minneapolis: Fortress, 2002.

———. *Luke the Theologian: Fifty-Five Years of Research (1950–2005)*. 2nd ed. Waco: Baylor University Press, 2006.

Brant, Jo-Ann A. *John*. Grand Rapids, MI: Baker Academic, 2011.

Bredin, Mark. *The Ecology of the New Testament: Creation, Re-Creation, and the Environment*. Colorado Springs: Biblica Publishing, 2010.

Brown, Jeannine K. *The Disciples in Narrative Perspective: The Portrayal and Function of the Matthean Disciples*. Atlanta: SBL, 2002.

Brown, Raymond E. *The Birth of the Messiah: A Commentary on the Infancy Narratives in Matthew and Luke*. New York: Doubleday, 1977.

Bruner, F. Dale. *The Gospel of John: A Commentary*. Grand Rapids, MI: Eerdmans, 2012.

Bultmann, Rudolf. *History of the Synoptic Tradition*. Oxford: Blackwell, 1963.

Burkett, Delbert. *The Son of Man Debate: A History and Evaluation*. Cambridge: Cambridge University Press, 1999.

Burridge, Richard A. *Four Gospels, One Jesus? A Symbolic Reading*. 2nd ed. Grand Rapids, MI: Eerdmans, 2005.

———. *What Are the Gospels? A Comparison with Graeco-Roman Biography*. 2nd ed. Grand Rapids, MI: Eerdmans, 2004.

Byrne, Brendan. *A Costly Freedom: A Theological Reading of Mark's Gospel*. Collegeville, MN: Liturgical Press, 2008.

———. *Life Abounding: A Reading of John's Gospel*. Collegeville, MN: Liturgical Press, 2014.

———. *Lifting the Burden: Reading Matthew's Gospel in the Church Today*. Collegeville, MN: Liturgical Press, 2004.

―――. *Romans*. Sacra Pagina 6. Collegeville, MN: Liturgical Press, 1996.

Carroll, John T. *Luke: A Commentary*. Louisville, KY: John Know Westminster, 2012.

Carter, Warren. *Matthew: Storyteller, Interpreter, Evangelist*. Peabody: Hendrickson, 2008.

The Cloud of Unknowing and Other Works. Penguin Classics, 2001.

Collins, Adela Yarbro. *Mark*. Hermeneia. Minneapolis: Augsburg Fortress, 2007.

Coloc, Mary E. "Theological Reflections on Creation in the Gospel of John." *Pacifica* 24 (2011): 1–12.

Culpepper, Gary. "'One suffering in two natures': An Analogical Inquiry into Divine and Human Suffering." In *Divine Impassibility and the Mystery of Human Suffering*, edited by James F. Keating and Thomas J. White, 77–98. Grand Rapids, MI: Eerdmans, 2009.

Culpepper, R. Alan. "Designs for the Church in the Imagery of John 21:1–14." In *Imagery in the Gospel of John: Terms, Forms, Themes, and Theology of Johannine Figurative Language*, edited by Jörge Frey, Jan van der Watt, and Ruben Zimmermann, 369–72. WUNT 200. Tübingen: Mohr Siebeck, 2006.

―――. *The Gospel and Letters of John*. Nashville: Abingdon, 1998.

Davies, W. D., and Dale C. Allison. *A Critical and Exegetical Commentary on the Gospel According to Saint Matthew*. 2 vols.; Edinburgh: T&T Clark, 1988.

―――. eds. *Matthew: A Shorter Commentary*. London: T & T Clark, 2004.

Edwards, Mark. *John through the Centuries*. BBC. Oxford: Blackwell, 2004.

Ehrmann, Bart D. "How the Problem of Pain Ruined My Faith," posted by N.T. Wright. http://www.beliefnet.com/columnists/blogalogue/2008/04/why-suffering-is-gods-problem.html.

―――. *The New Testament: A Historical Introduction to the Early Christian Writings*. 4th ed.; New York: Oxford University Press, 2008.

Eusebius, *Ecclesiastical History*.

Fitzmyer, Joseph A. *The Gospel According to Luke*. 2 vols. New York: Doubleday, 1979.

Focant, Camille. *The Gospel According to Mark: A Commentary*. Eugene: Pickwick, 2012.

France, R. T. *The Gospel of Mark. A Commentary on the Greek Text*. NIGNTC. Grand Rapids, MI: Eerdmans, 2002.

Frankl, Viktor E. *Man's Search for Meaning*. 4th ed. Boston: Beacon Press, 1992.

Furedi, Frank. *Culture of Fear Revisited: Risk-Taking and the Morality of Low Expectation*. 4th ed. London/New York: Continuum, 2006.

González, Justo L. *Luke*. Belief. Louisville, KY: Westminster John Knox, 2010.

Goodacre, Mark S., and Nicholas Perrin, eds. *Questioning Q*. London: SPCK, 2004.

———. "Ten Reasons to Question Q," http://www.markgoodacre.org/Q/ten.htm.

Graham, Kenneth. *The Wind in the Willows*. London: Book Club Associates, 1977.

Gray, Timothy C. *The Temple in the Gospel of Mark: A Study in Its Narrative Role*. Grand Rapids, MI: Baker Academic, 2008.

Green, Joel B. *The Gospel of Luke*. NICNT. Grand Rapids, MI: Eerdmans, 1997.

Green, Joel B., and Lee Martin McDonald, eds. *The World of the New Testament: Cultural, Social, and Historical Contexts*. Grand Rapids, MI: Baker Academic, 2013.

Hagner, Donald A. *Matthew 1–13*. World Biblical Commentary. Nashville: Thomas Nelson, 2000.

Hanson, Rick. *Buddha's Brain: The Practical Neuroscience of Happiness, Love and Wisdom*. Oakland, CA: New Harbinger Publications, 2009.

Harrington, Wilfrid J. *Reading Luke for the First Time*. Mahwah, NJ: Paulist Press, 1997.

Hart, David Bentley. *The Beauty of the Infinite: The Aesthetics of Christian Truth*. Grand Rapids, MI: Eerdmans, 2003 e-book.

———. *The Doors of the Sea: Where Was God in the Tsunami*. Grand Rapids, MI: Eerdmans, 2005 e-book.

Hengel, Martin. *Saint Peter: The Underestimated Apostle*. Grand Rapids, MI: Eerdmans, 2010.

———. *Studies in the Gospel of Mark*. London: SCM, 1985.

Holmas, Geir O. *Prayer and Vindication in Luke-Acts*. LNT. London: Bloomsbury, 2011.

Hooker, Morna A. *The Gospel According to Saint Mark*. London: A & C Black, 1991.

Irenaeus, *Against Heresies*, in Cyril Richardson, *Early Christian Fathers*. New York, NY: Touchstone, 1996.

Iverson, Kelly R., and Christopher W. Skinner, eds. *Mark as Story: Retrospect and Prospect*. Atlanta: SBL, 2011.

Johnson, Luke Timothy. *The Gospel of Luke*. Sacra Pagina 3. Collegeville, MN: Liturgical Press, 1991.

Johnson, Philip. "Dear Brittany: Our Lives Are Worth Living, Even with Brain Cancer." The Catholic Diocese of Raleigh. http://www.dioceseofraleigh.org/content/raleigh-seminarian-terminal-brain-cancer-responds-brittany-maynard.

Josephus, *The Jewish War*. Penguin Classics, 1981, Kindle edition.

Julian of Norwich. *Revelations of Divine Love*. London: Hodder & Stoughton, 1987.

Just, Arthur A. *Luke*. 2 vols. St. Louis: Concordia Publishing House, 1997.

Keener, Craig S. *The Gospel of John: A Commentary*. Peabody: Hendrickson, 2003.

King, Geoffrey. "Life or Death Decision Inspired by Faith in God." *The Age*. April 4, 2013.

Köestenberger, Andrea J. *John*. BECNT. Grand Rapids, MI: Baker Academic, 2004.

Kovacs, Judith. "'Now Shall the Ruler of This World Be Driven Out': Jesus' Death as Cosmic Battle in John 12:30–36." *Journal of Biblical Literature* 111 (1995): 227–47.

Kupp, David D. *Matthew's Emmanuel: Divine Presence and God's People in the First Gospel*. Cambridge: Cambridge University Press, 1996.

Kysar, Robert. *John the Maverick Gospel*. 3rd ed. Louisville, KY: Westminster John Knox, 2007.

Lee, Dorothy A. *Flesh and Glory: Symbol, Gender and Theology in the Gospel of John*. New York: Crossroad, 2002.

———. *Hallowed in Truth and Love: Spirituality in the Johannine Literature*. Melbourne/Eugene: Mosaic/Wipf & Stock, 2011–12.

———. *Transfiguration*. London and New York: Continuum, 2004.

———. "Witness in the Fourth Gospel: John the Baptist and the Beloved Disciple as Counterparts." *Australian Biblical Review* 61 (2013): 1–17.

Lewis, C. S. *A Grief Observed*. London: Faber & Faber, 1961.

———. *The Problem of Pain*. New York: Macmillan, 1944.

———. "The Weight of Glory," sermon preached at St. Mary the Virgin, Oxford, June 8, 1942. http://www.verber.com/mark/xian/weight-of-glory.pdf.

Lincoln, Andrew T. *The Gospel According to Saint John*. BNTC. London: Continuum, 2005.

Luz, Ulrich. *Matthew: A Commentary*. 3 vols. Hermeneia. Minneapolis: Fortress, 2005–7.

Malangu, Elijah. "The Ancient Mediterranean Values of Honour and Shame as a Hermeneutical Procedure." *Verbum et Ecclesia* 22 (2001): 85–101.

Malbon, Elizabeth S. *Mark's Jesus: Characterization as Narrative Christology*. Waco: Baylor University, 2009.

Marcus, Joel. *Mark 1–8: A New Translation with Introduction and Commentary*. New York: Doubleday, 2000.

———. *Mark 8–16: A New Translation with Introduction and Commentary*. New Haven and London: Yale University Press, 2009.

Matera, Frank J. *Romans*. Paideia. Grand Rapids, MI: Baker Academic, 2010.

de Mello, Anthony. *Sadhana, a Way to God: Christian Exercises in Eastern Form*. New York: Doubleday, 1978.

Middleton, J. Richard. *The Liberating Image: The Imago Dei in Genesis 1*. Grand Rapids, MI: Brazos Press, 2005.

Minear, Paul S. *Matthew: The Teacher's Gospel*. London: Darton, Longman and Todd, 1982.

Moloney, Francis J. *The Gospel of John*. Sacra Pagina. Collegeville, MN: Liturgical Press, 1998.

———. *The Gospel of Mark: A Commentary*. Peabody: Hendrickson, 2002.

———. "John 21 and the Johannine Story." In *Anatomies of Narrative Criticism: The Past, Present, and Futures of the Fourth Gospel as Literature*, edited by Tom Thatcher and Stephen D. Moore, 237–51. Atlanta: SBL, 2008.

————. *Love in the Gospel of John: An Exegetical, Theological, and Literary Study.* Grand Rapids, MI: Baker Academic, 2013.

————. *The Resurrection of the Messiah: A Narrative Commentary on the Resurrection Accounts in the Four Gospels.* New York: Paulist Press, 2013.

————. "Writing a Narrative Commentary on the Gospel of Mark." In *Mark as Story: Retrospect and Prospect,* edited by Kelly Iverson and Christopher W. Skinner, 95–114. Atlanta: SBL, 2011.

Neyrey, Jerome H. "What's Wrong with This Picture? John 4, Cultural Stereotypes of Women, and Public and Private Space." In *A Feminist Companion to John,* edited by Amy-Jill Levine, 1:98–125. 2 vols. London: Sheffield Academic Press, 2003.

Orsillo, Susan M., and Lizabeth Roemer. *The Mindful Way through Anxiety.* New York: Guildford Press, 2011.

Painter, John. *The Quest for the Messiah: The History, Literature and Theology of the Johannine Community.* Edinburgh: T&T Clark, 1991.

Parsons, Mikeal C. *Luke.* Paideia. Grand Rapids, MI: Baker Academic, 2015.

Pennington, Jonathan T. *Heaven and Earth in the Gospel of Matthew.* Leiden/Boston: Brill, 2007.

Perkins, Pheme. *Reading the New Testament: An Introduction.* 3rd ed. Mahwah, NJ: Paulist Press, 2012.

Pieris, Aloysius. "Spirituality as Mindfulness: Biblical and Buddhist Approaches." *Spiritus: A Journal of Christian Spirituality* 10, no. 1 (2010).

Polkinghorne, John C., and Nicholas Beale. *Questions of Truth: Fifty-One Responses to Questions about God, Science, and Belief.* Louisville, KY: Westminster John Knox Press, 2009.

Powell, Mark Allan. *Fortress Introduction to the Gospels.* Minneapolis: Augsburg Fortress, 1998.

A Prayer Book for Australia. Melbourne: Broughton Publishing, 1995.

Rhoads, David. "Overall Care for Creation: Reflections on the Gospel of Luke in Year C for Preaching and Devotion." http://www.lutheransrestoringcreation.org/overall-care-for

-creation-reflections-on-the-gospel-of-luke-in-year-c-for
-preaching-and-devotion.

———. *Reading Mark: Engaging the Gospel*. Minneapolis: Fortress, 2004.

Richards, E. Randolph. "Reading, Writing, and Manuscripts." In
*The World of the New Testament: Cultural, Social, and Historical
Contexts*, edited by Joel B. Green and Lee Martin McDonald,
345–66. Grand Rapids, MI: Baker Academic, 2013.

Roosevelt, Franklin D. First Inaugural Address as President of
the USA. http://historymatters.gmu.edu/d/5057/.

Saint Augustine. *The Confessions*. Translated by M. Boulding. 2nd
ed. New York: New City Press, 2014.

Schnackenburg, Rudolf. *The Gospel According to St. John*. 3 vols.
London: Burns and Oates, 1980.

Senior, Donald. *Matthew*. ANTC. Nashville: Abingdon, 1998.

Sloan, David. "The Case for Q." http://www.umass.edu/wsp/
alpha/forum/luke/2014e%20Sloan%20Q%20abs.pdf.

von Speyr, Adrianne. *Mark: Meditations for a Community*. San
Francisco: Ignatius Press, 2012.

Spufford, Francis. *Unapologetic: Why, Despite Everything, Christianity Can Still Make Surprising Emotional Sense*. London:
Faber & Faber, 2012.

St. James, Rebecca. *Sister Freaks: Stories of Women Who Gave Up
Everything for God*. New York: Alive Communications, 2005.

Tannehill, Robert C. "The Disciples in Mark: The Function of
a Narrative Role." In *The Interpretation of Mark*, edited by
William R. Telford, 169–95. 2nd ed.; Edinburgh: T&T Clark,
1995.

———. *The Narrative Unity of Luke-Acts: A Literary Interpretation*.
Minneapolis: Fortress, 1986.

Telford, William R. *Writing on the Gospel of Mark*. Blandford
Forum: Deo Publishing, 2009.

Tillich, Paul. *The Courage to Be*. London: Fontana, 1952.

Tuckett, Christopher M. *Luke*. Sheffield: Sheffield Academic
Press, 1996.

Vinson, Richard. *Luke*. Macon: Smyth & Helwys, 2008.

Welby, Justin. "Standing Room Only - Interview with Archbishop Justin Welby." https://www.youtube.com/watch?v=
exmHYXNEt9A&feature=youtu.be&t=11m52s.

Westminster Abbey website: http://www.westminster-abbey .org/our-history/people/manche-masemola.

Wilde, Oscar. *Collected Works of Oscar Wilde: The Complete Plays, Poems and Stories*. Ware, Hertfordshire: Wordsworth Editions, 1997.

Williams, W. K. *Galatians*. Nashville: Abingdon, 1997.

Winterson, Jeanette. "Why We Need Fairy Tales: Jeanette Winterson on Oscar Wilde," *The Guardian*. October 17, 2013. http://www.theguardian.com/books/2013/oct/16/jeanette -winterson-fairytales-oscar-wilde.

Wright, Archie T. "Jewish Identity, Beliefs, and Practices." In *The World of the New Testament: Cultural, Social and Historical Contexts*, edited by Joel B. Green and Lee Martin McDonald, 318–21. Grand Rapids, MI: Baker, 2013.

Zeidan, Fadel, et al., "Neural Correlates of Mindfulness Meditation-Related Anxiety Relief," *Journal of Social Cognitive and Affective Neuroscience* (June 3, 2013): 1–9.

Zizioulas, John. "Proprietors or Priests of Creation." In *Toward an Ecology of Transfiguration: Orthodox Christian Perspectives on Environment, Nature, and Creation*, edited by John Chryssavgis and Bruce V. Foltz, 163–71. New York: Fordham University Press, 2013.

Zweig, Connie. *The Holy Longing: Spiritual Yearning and Its Shadow Side*. Bloomington: iUniverse, 2008, e-book.